The
Open Door

The
Open Door

INSPIRING AND MIRACULOUS STORIES FROM YOUTH EVANGELISTS

Compiled by Kamil Metz

This book was
Edited by Laura Wehr and Joelle Worf
Copyedited by Tim Lale
Designed by John Yoon

Devotionals at the beginning of each chapter by
Mark Howard, Emmanuel Institute of Evangelism (www.emmanuelinstitute.org).

ISBN: 978-0-692-32283-3

Additional copies of this book may be purchased at http://www.theopendoorbook.com.

18 17 16 15 14   •   5 4 3 2 1

Dedication

K. Dick Thomas

For rallying around the idea of printing the first magabook, *He Taught Love*, and thus starting a movement of *new* student literature evangelists who have had an impact on millions through the magabook LE ministry. What a great loss it would have been if that first magabook had never been printed!

Contents

Foreword ▶ 9

1: Messengers of Hope ▶ 13

2: God's Providence ▶ 27

3: The Great Controversy ▶ 39

4: He Answers ▶ 54

5: Power of Persistence ▶ 66

6: God's Timing ▶ 85

7: Angels Among Us ▶ 99

8: Other Ways to Reach Souls ▶ 111

9: The Invisible Helper ▶ 125

10: His Faithfulness ▶ 140

Foreword

The book you're holding in your hands is one of the most remarkable books you'll ever read. It is a book of miracles involving young people, the Holy Spirit, and a willingness to be used by God, to be involved in His work.

Evangelism is God's work. It is the work that God wants everyone to be involved in. And it is a work that takes many forms. The youth evangelists you read about in this book have participated in a very special form of ministry—literature evangelism.

Everywhere you go, people are looking toward heaven—people with a void in their lives that can only be filled by the presence of Jesus Christ. Literature evangelists start each day of ministry understanding the infinite possibilities that lie before them—the possibility of miracles, the possibility of divine appointments, the possibility of transformation, the possibility of salvation occurring in a life that was seemingly without hope.

You might be tempted, as you read the stories in this book, to say, "That could never happen." If that's your reaction when you read about a book that would not burn after it was thrown into a fire, I understand fully. When you read about the young woman who was planning to end her life but prayed one final, desperate prayer before encountering a youth evangelist and finding Jesus, you might be tempted to say, "No way!" You might be tempted to doubt the veracity of these stories.

But I don't doubt them for a moment. Nobody who has been a literature evangelist would doubt these stories, because literature evangelists understand that God is in the miracle-working business. I *have been a literature evangelist*. Never have I heard the voice of God more clearly than when I was involved in canvassing.

After a long but satisfying day in the field, I was driving home when I sensed the voice of God say to me, "Go back!" I had just driven past two houses, one on either side of the road. At one, I had seen an elderly couple sitting on the porch. At the other, a young family—Mom, Dad and two children—playing in the front yard. I wasn't interested in going back. It was time to go home.

But something said, "Go back, and go to the *elderly couple*," which didn't make sense. Young families are more likely to get books. I chased the impression out of my mind twice, but on the third impression I pulled into a driveway and said out loud to God, "OK, I'll go back. I really think I'm making a mistake here, but just in case this is from You, I'll go back." And you know what happened? I walked up the small incline toward the couple on their front porch, and one of them said to me, "Hey there! What's that you have for us?" And did they ever get books! A whole lot!

Another time, a group of us student literature evangelists went out for dinner. This was a rare treat. We were poor students, but we decided to splurge and eat well. At the restaurant, one person in our group decided to tell the waitress what we were doing in town. Noticing she was interested, another person in the group ran to the van and brought back an armload of books. Next, a third person described the books to her, a fourth closed, and finally the fifth wrote the receipt for her donation! The waitress got an armload of books, and God bought dinner for us all!

Literature evangelism is exciting! Evangelism is exciting. Being on the front lines with God is exhilarating. Seeing God work in a life, being used by God to impact a life, is a thrill that can't be beaten. The youth evangelists you'll read about in this book understand that literature ministry isn't simply a matter of getting books out. It's a matter of sharing Jesus and winning souls. Imagine going out to work for the day and being used by God to share the light of the Bible with a man who *just* that morning had prayed about his growing conviction to keep the Sabbath day holy! Or imagine the thrill of discovering you had just spent an afternoon canvassing with an angel—a real angel—as your ministry partner!

Incredible? Yes. But then God is incredible. Unbelievable? To some people, certainly. But not to someone who has spent time being used by God as a literature evangelist to reach souls for His glory.

I know you'll be inspired as you read *The Open Door*. And I pray you'll not only be inspired by the example and experience of others, but that you'll be inspired to pray for divine appointments, and to be used by God in some way to reach others for His kingdom.

May God bless you!

John Bradshaw
Speaker/Director, *It Is Written* television ministry
(and former youth literature evangelist)

1

Messengers of Hope

"How beautiful are the feet of those who preach the gospel of peace, who bring glad tidings of good things!" (Romans 10:15).

In the days of Elijah the prophet, God instructed him to go to Zarephath because, He said, " 'I have commanded a widow there to provide for you' " (1 Kings 17:9). The curious thing is that the widow didn't seem to know anything about it! In fact, when Elijah arrived, she was gathering sticks to make one last fire to cook a meal for herself and her son so that, she said, "we may eat it, and die" (v. 12).

The prophet then encouraged her not to fear, but to first make a meal for him, because Jehovah, the God of Israel, had promised that "the bin of flour shall not be used up, nor shall the jar of oil run dry, until the day the Lord sends rain on the earth" (v. 14). This was a severe test of faith, but she did as the prophet said, and "she and he and her household ate for many days" (v. 15).

Though neither the prophet nor the widow were aware of it, the Lord was intimately acquainted with the plight of this poor woman and her son, and sent

His messenger at just the right moment to bring encouragement and hope, and to connect her with the source of hope.

In our day, multitudes of people are longing for something better, "having no hope and without God in the world" (Ephesians 2:12). God sends His servants as messengers of hope into these dark and gloomy places to introduce them to the Light of life. We are told in the book *The Desire of Ages*, "We are to minister to the despairing, and inspire hope in the hopeless" (350). Why not choose today to be a messenger of hope for Jesus?

He *had* wanted her

One afternoon, Maribel Ramos decided to bring her Bible with her as she canvassed door to door. When her leader dropped her off on a new street, he directed her to start with the *third* house and specifically said, "Something powerful is about to happen."

After praying for a divine appointment alone on the sidewalk, she built up the confidence to knock on the door. A woman answered. Maribel had hardly begun showing her a cookbook when the woman interjected that she wasn't interested and closed the door on her rather abruptly.

Maribel stood there, bewildered, remembering what her leader had told her. However, before she had very long to consider what had just happened—or rather what had not happened—the door reopened five seconds after it had closed, and a younger woman appeared who seemed genuinely interested in why she was at the door.

As she canvassed, Maribel noticed that the young woman, Sophia, wasn't interested in either the cookbook or the children's book, but when Maribel handed her the devotional book *Man of Peace*, her eyes showed immediate interest. She pulled Maribel to the driveway to prevent her family from hearing their conversation.

Sophia held the book close to her chest as she confessed, "Last night I wanted to take my life, and as I was smoking in this very driveway, talking to the sky as if God could hear me, I said, 'God, if You're really *real* and want to know me, You will send someone to me, or else my life ends tomorrow.' "

With chills running down her spine and tears filling her eyes, Maribel smiled a broad smile as she listened to Sophia's story.

"It's no coincidence that you're here today!" Sophia finished. The girls hugged each other tightly, knowing God had answered Sophia's prayer.

Sophia filled out the Bible study form immediately, and the Holy Spirit told Maribel to give Sophia her own personal Bible. After she prayed, Maribel says, she "left the house amazed and humbled, knowing that the God of the universe had allowed me to be sent as His ambassador, to save His lost child from both physical and spiritual death." Amazing love! He *had* wanted her.

"Are you an angel?"

Kristina Reeves bounced into the van, slamming the door with a bang.

"Businesses are so much fun, Cestmir!"

Cestmir, her colporteur leader, smiled at her enthusiasm as he drove toward another street where they would work. They drove past more businesses and then, to her surprise, pulled into a quiet neighborhood. It looked quite deserted, and there were only a few houses on one side of the street. Her heart sank. She had been looking forward to doing a few more businesses.

"Kristina," Cestmir's voice broke through her thoughts, "start at this house and go down the street until you meet Tammy. It's nearly time for lunch." Swallowing her disappointment, she jumped out of the van and raced to the first house, waving goodbye as the van sped away.

No one was home. At the next house, again no one was home. Trudging toward the next house, she silently pleaded, "God, why did you send me here? Cestmir never puts me in houses before lunch. And besides, I was doing so well in business- es this morning!"

At last, she came to a house where the door was open. Through the screen door she could see a young woman sitting in the living room.

"Hello!" she called to the woman.

Slowly the woman came to the door, her face filled with hopelessness.

When she saw the first book, a cookbook, the woman immediately turned away. "I'm not interested," she mumbled, walking back toward her living room.

Instantly a strong impression came over Kristina. *Ask her if she likes to read.*

No! she argued within herself. *She just said she wasn't interested!*

But the nagging impression was insistent: *Ask her if she likes to read.*

Clearing her throat, Kristina relented, and spoke to the retreating figure, "Excuse me, ma'am, do you like to read?"

The woman turned around and came back to the door. "Yes," she answered, "sometimes."

Surprised by the woman's renewed interest, Kristina reached into her bag for a book and instinctively pulled out a *Peace Above the Storm*. Then she heard herself share the canvass: "This is a beautiful devotional that will help you find freedom from worry, guilt, and fear."

The screen door opened and the young woman, with tears trickling down her cheeks, took the book from Kristina's outstretched hand. "My husband left me this morning. For good," she said quietly between sobs. "I'm not a Christian. I don't know much about God. But I was in my living room, and I said, 'God, if you're really there, if you don't do something for me right now, I'm going to break down.' At that moment you knocked at my door."

She looked up at Kristina. "Now I know that God is real and He really does answer prayers! He's the one who told you to show me this second book, and He must want me to get it!"

With those words, the young woman hurried back inside to find her purse. She gave her last dollars to Kristina as a donation for the *Peace Above the Storm*, and Kristina read an encouraging quotation to her and prayed for her. As their prayer ended, the woman looked searchingly at Kristina.

"Are you sure you're not an angel?" she asked.

As Kristina left the home and continued down the street, every trace of disappointment was gone. She recalls, "God had used me in ways I never dreamed possible!"

When Cestmir arrived later to pick her up for their lunch break, Kristina excitedly told him the story. He became quiet for a moment as a funny smile flickered across his face.

"You know, I had another street of businesses all picked out for you," he confessed, "but, somehow, on our way there, I had this impression to drop you off on this street instead. I didn't know why, but now I'm glad I did!"

Please use my hands

While knocking on doors in an apartment building, Jonathan Zita met a man whose appearance was appalling. Many of his teeth had fallen out, and he was visibly sick.

His legs were so weak that he could only stand for brief periods. Yet in spite of his physical condition, Stefan had a smile on his face. He was interested in the books Jonathan was offering, and the two began to visit.

As Stefan shared about his life, Jonathan at first felt sorry for him. He had a fatal disease, his wife had left him with their child, and his doctor told him that he wouldn't live to see his son graduate from elementary school. He was stuck at home, just waiting to die. Why would a man with such terrible problems still smile?

"I praise the Lord even in my sickness!" Stefan told Jonathan. "If it wasn't for my illness, I probably would never have known Him."

Stefan was excited about prophecy and decided to get *The Great Controversy*. Before leaving, Jonathan asked if he could pray for him. When Jonathan had finished his prayer, Stefan prayed a prayer that brought tears to Jonathan's eyes.

"Lord, I pray for healing, that I may serve You like these young people. And even if You don't heal me, Lord, please use me still. You took away my legs, my health, my family, and my future, but I still have my hands. Here are my hands, Lord. If You can, please use my hands to do something more for You."

When Jonathan left Stefan's home that night, he no longer felt sorry for him. Instead, his heart was sad over the thousands of young people who do have their legs, their hands, and their future ahead of them, but won't do anything for God. Yet here was this man who echoed Job's own words: "Though He slay me, yet will I trust Him" (Job 13:15).

"God," Jonathan prayed as he drove, "please use my hands too. But not only my hands, Lord—please use everything I have for Your service."

Some time later, Jonathan was surprised to meet Stefan again—this time at an evangelistic meeting at Jonathan's church.

"Jonathan, I want you to know that prayer really works!" Stefan said.

"What do you mean?" Jonathan asked.

"God has been healing me! Now I am able to serve Him more! You must tell your church that God answers prayers!"

From humor to humility

Renee Edwards saw up ahead a group of friends in their fifties and sixties, sitting on a patio. Feeling nervous about approaching an entire group, Renee prayed as she walked, asking God for strength. She greeted the group and then handed a book to a woman sitting in the middle.

Flipping the cookbook open, the woman joked, "Are there any recipes in here for bachelors?"

A wave of laughter spread through the group of friends. The woman continued joking, but the subject matter wasn't funny: she was dying of cancer. Renee noticed the wine and cigarettes on the table nearby and thought to herself that the woman's bravado was just an attempt at coping with her situation. Taking a chance, Renee handed her *Peace Above the Storm*. The book fell open to the chapter titled, "Discovering Peace of Mind." The woman's expression changed, and tears came to her eyes. As Renee shared about the book, tears began to trickle down her face as well.

"How much?" the woman asked, interrupting Renee.

"Some people help with as close to ten dollars as they can," Renee managed to say.

"Honey!" the woman shouted, "Get twenty dollars!" Turning back to Renee, she asked, "What else do you have? I want to be humble before I go. Do you have anything that will help me to be humble?"

Renee left her with *Peace above the Storm* as well as *Man of Peace*. Before heading to the next door, Renee prayed with the woman, and by the time she left, the entire group was tearful.

Renee recalls, "I *knew* that God sent me there right on time—right before it was too late for her. The Lord used me to give her another chance to come to Him, another chance to be 'humble,' as she called it, and repent before her Maker." And what a precious promise the humble can claim: "Humble yourselves in the sight of the Lord, and He will lift you up" (James 4:10).

Come back!

Jennita Schmidt was leaving a grocery store when she spotted a young female employee sitting on a bench outside the store. Though the store managers had shown little interest in Jennita's books, Jennita decided to speak to the woman on her work break. The woman took an immediate interest in her books and selected *God's Answers to Your Questions* and *Peace Above the Storm*. Jennita quickly went on her way to the other stores in the plaza, praising God for His divine timing in allowing her to meet that particular employee.

Later, as Jennita finished visiting the stores, she decided to cross the grocery store parking lot again on her way to the next shopping center.

"Hey, come back!" someone called out.

Jennita looked around, surprised, and spotted the woman from the grocery store running toward her.

"Can you please come back?" the woman called again. "We've been looking all over for you. The ladies in the kitchen saw my books, and they want books too!"

Back inside the grocery store, several women greeted Jennita enthusiastically. Quite a few of them wanted books from her, and the next few moments were filled with a flurry of activity as Jennita handed her books around and filled out donation receipts for each of them. Then, as the other women returned to their work, Jennita looked up and saw one more woman waiting to talk to her.

"May I see the book on peace?" she asked.

"Of course!" Jennita said, handing her the picture-filled *Peace Above the Storm*.

"You have no idea the storms I am going through right now, and it seems like things are just getting worse. Yesterday, my car blew a tire, and I completely lost control." Charlotte explained how her car had careened off the road, missing ditches and trees by mere inches.

"I know it's a miracle of God that I'm alive today," she acknowledged. "But even so, I just don't know how I can survive all the other storms in my life right now! I was just praying yesterday, 'Oh, God, help me find peace. Help me somehow.' And then my co-worker showed me this book—*Peace Above the Storm*." Tears streamed down Charlotte's cheeks as she continued. "I knew it was no coincidence. But when the others went looking for you, they couldn't find you anywhere. God must have brought you back."

Jennita was sure she could feel God's presence surrounding them there in the aisles of the busy grocery store as she opened the book and shared some of her favorite encouraging quotations with Charlotte.

"You just can't know how much it means to me that you came back," Charlotte said, giving Jennita a big hug.

And isn't it encouraging to know that Jesus, who "is our peace," is coming back for us too? (Ephesians 2:14).

When facing failure

It was unusually hot as Hillary Barrett worked her way down a residential street. Though she had been claiming Bible promises in an effort to keep her spirits up, the oppressive heat and the empty homes seemed to drain the energy and cheer right out of her. As she approached an intersection, she came upon a few businesses, and her heart sank even further. As a new canvasser, Hillary was still afraid of meeting people while they were at work.

"Lord," she prayed, "please bless me with a divine appointment! I need a positive experience to keep me encouraged."

As she stepped into the air-conditioned cool of a small convenience store, she was met with a discouraging sight. Between her and the cashier stood a long line of people! Taking a deep breath, she pushed her fears aside and pressed her way to the front.

She tried to explain what she was doing to the busy cashier, but he only gave her a quick sideways glance and held up a finger to indicate that she needed to wait.

Should I stay? Hillary began to wonder. *He looks so busy. Perhaps I should just go . . .* But before she could decide what to do, the man called over another cashier to take his place and motioned her to a quiet corner of the store.

Hillary showed the man her books, and after he decided to get four spiritual books, he pulled out a Bible.

"Let me share a verse with you that I read this morning. I think it will help you in your important work," he said, turning the pages of his Bible to 1 Samuel 30:6. "Now David was greatly distressed, for the people spoke of stoning him, because the soul of all the people was grieved, every man for his sons and his daughters. But David strengthened himself in the Lord his God.' Hillary, as Christians doing God's work, we can't wait for circumstances to cheer us up or encourage us. We have to be like David and make up our mind to strengthen ourselves in the Lord, even in the face of complete failure!"

Then, to Hillary's great surprise, the clerk offered to pray for her. She gratefully accepted, and followed his prayer with one of her own, expressing her thankfulness for God's patience with her flagging spirits and for His blessing in the form of this convenience store clerk.

Hillary recalls, "The lesson I learned that day is to encourage myself in the Lord, no matter the circumstance!"

Tested like Job

When Melissa Allen knocked on Annette's door, Annette was out of money and struggling with major health issues. Although she was interested in the picture-filled *Peace Above the Storm*, she just couldn't afford it.

"Can you come back next week?" she asked. "I'll get the books then!"

But Melissa knew that she couldn't come back. Instead, she offered Annette a pocket-sized version. As Annette went back inside to find a few dollars, she invited Melissa in for a drink of water.

Once inside, Annette turned to Melissa. "Why does God allow bad things to happen to good people? I know I haven't been the best person, but is God really punishing me?"

Melissa took a deep breath and cried out silently to God for wisdom. "May I tell you a story about a man in the Bible who could have asked the same question? His name is Job."

As Melissa related Job's story, Annette's expression changed. Before Melissa could finish, Annette interrupted.

"I get it! I get it! I stopped following Satan's ways and now Satan is trying to get me to come back. I am being tested."

As they continued to talk, calmness came over Annette. Over and over, she thanked Melissa for coming, and even called their encounter a divine appointment. Before parting, Annette signed up for Bible studies with the local church, and they exchanged phone numbers.

A few days later, Annette called Melissa with an update. She wanted Melissa to know that she was continuing to follow God and that He was blessing her for her faithfulness. Annette had learned that while she might be "grieved by various trials," the genuineness of her faith was "much more precious than gold" (1 Peter 1:6, 7).

Full circle

Sandra Conway approached a door, knocked, and waited. After a few moments, the door swung open, and a woman appeared. "Hello, my name is Sandra, and I'm a student working on a scholarship program." With that, Sandra launched into her presentation, the newest member of an old ministry that had transformed her own life just a few years before.

Sandra was raised in the Catholic Church and attended services with her mother. Her father had also been a Catholic, but he had left the faith, and also the family, a long time before. Since then, it had been just Sandra and her mother, supporting each other and holding on to the only faith they had ever known. But as life's difficulties mounted, they too began to doubt. Is God good? If He even exists, can He be trusted? As their doubts increased, Sandra and her mother began to separate themselves from the church and finally let go of their faith in God altogether.

By the time Sandra turned 15, she had been out of the church for almost four years. But that year, with a rekindled interest in spirituality and a curiosity about the Bible, Sandra began to study the Bible for the first time in her life. Then one afternoon, while Sandra wasn't home, someone knocked on her front door. Her mother answered the door and was greeted by a young man and a woman, both with books in hand. The two were student literature evangelists, and that initial introduction began a friendship between Sandra, her mother, and the two colporteurs, Jonathan and Dora. Sandra and her mother were open to Bible studies, so Dora and Jonathan visited regularly. They spent many moments together in Sandra's kitchen talking and sharing together as friends, and over the course of these visits, Sandra learned more about God, the Bible, and the Adventist faith. She even began to go door to door with Dora, serving as an active prayer partner in the ministry. Then, at the age of 18, Sandra gave her life to Jesus and was baptized into the Seventh-day Adventist Church.

Soon afterward, Sandra decided to attend Canadian University College in Alberta, Canada. While there, Sandra learned about a student literature evangelism summer ministry from someone who was already in the program. Excited about this opportunity to win souls for Christ, she joined the program and began knocking on doors.

Sandra knocked on many doors that summer and learned lessons about patience, perseverance, and complete dependence on God. Her story demonstrates the power of a single knock to impact not just one life, but many others. She received to give—an unbroken circle, reflecting the light, joy, and hope she now lives.

A silent communion of strangers

A little girl, riding her bike through her neighborhood, grew curious as she passed an older girl carrying a bag of books. Circling back to pass her again, she called out in broken English. "What are you doing?"

"I'm sharing these books with your neighbors," Hillary Blair answered, "and their donations help me earn scholarship money for school."

Hopping off her bike, the little girl offered to introduce Hillary to her aunt. When the aunt was unable to help, the little girl went back inside the house. "I'll get my mother!" she told Hillary.

Hillary was a bit nervous as she waited. She knew that the mother probably didn't speak English. And what might the mother think of her daughter talking to a stranger of a different religion in the street? In addition, Hillary was there to offer books in return for a donation! Would the mother be annoyed?

However, as soon as Hillary saw the mother coming through the door, she felt at peace. Though the mother didn't speak English, the little girl's eyes danced with delight and accomplishment, as she was able to translate Hillary's words. The girl was genuinely disappointed when her mother explained that they wouldn't be able to help.

"That's OK," Hillary told the girl. The mother, recognizing the word *OK*, smiled at Hillary. As Hillary smiled back, she felt that despite their differences, the three of them were sharing a silent communion. After a few moments, Hillary spoke, breaking the strange peace.

"I can't leave without giving you this book." Turning to the little girl, she handed her a pamphlet version of *Steps to Christ*. "I know you like to read English." Then, with many nods and smiles, the three said their goodbyes.

For days after the encounter, Hillary found herself thinking about the little girl, Ramya. Ramya lived in poverty. She was a foreigner. She spoke English in broken phrases. She had been by herself on her bike, and Hillary was very different from her. Nevertheless, Ramya initiated conversation and offered her assistance to a stranger, resulting in an unexpected and beautiful moment of fellowship shared by strangers. Though Ramya wasn't a Christian, Hillary felt that she had been an example of Christian love to her.

"If that were me as a child," Hillary recalls, "I would have kept riding my bike and only given a quick, suspicious smile to the girl with the bag of books. We so often let our circumstances dictate our ability to truly care for others, but it wasn't so with Ramya. I see in her the Christian that I want to be, and she wasn't even a Christian! In Sanskrit, Ramya means 'beautiful,' and that's what she was—a little girl with a beautiful heart. Isn't that what a Christian should be?"

Indeed, Jesus Himself said, "Unless you are converted and become as little children, you will by no means enter the kingdom of heaven." "For of such is the kingdom of heaven" (Matthew 18:3, 19:14). In fact, Hillary has faith that the little girl with the beautiful heart will read the pamphlet version of *Steps to Christ* and meet the One who has already been working in her heart.

Hidden gems

One day Raluca Ancu led a team of youth canvassing in a town near Orlando, Florida, that she had not intended on going to, but which resulted in great blessings!

Nicki, a student canvasser, knocked on a door, and the woman said she was not interested. Nicki acknowledged that and offered instead to pray for her. So she prayed for the woman and then shared a pamphlet version of *Steps to Christ*. The woman looked at the booklet and then asked, "Could I see your books again?" She ended up choosing *God's Answers to Your Questions* and signed up for Bible studies.

Raluca's primary role that summer was not that of youth canvassing leader, however, but of Bible worker. She ended up going back to the home of that woman and studying with her.

We are told that "many are on the verge of the kingdom, waiting only to be gathered in" (*The Acts of the Apostles, 109*), and that was just what Raluca found. As she visited and started to study with the woman, the Holy Spirit began to move on her heart. She had lots of questions about the Sabbath but nevertheless continued to study.

When evangelistic meetings in Orlando started, Raluca invited her to come, and she came! The woman then suggested that her aunt, a Sunday school teacher at her church, come, and she came too. They began learning many new truths. Before long, a local conference evangelist went with Raluca to visit the woman and her aunt. Since the aunt was a leader at her church, and leaving one's church can be very challenging, they spent extra time with her, highlighting the Bible truths that were being presented and the need to follow all of God's truth.

When Pastor Mark Finley made appeals for people to surrender their lives fully to Christ, the dear woman and her aunt responded and made the decision to be baptized.

What a joy it was for Raluca and Nicki to see both of them baptized!

Close enough to hear

"Come in!" a voice called from inside.

"Are you sure?" Jennita Schmidt answered back. "I'm Jennita, a student working on a scholarship program."

"Yes, come in!" the voice responded.

Slowly, Jennita opened the apartment door on which she had just knocked. Peering inside, she saw an older woman seated in an armchair. Kneeling down beside the chair, Jennita pulled out her books to share with the woman. When she saw *Peace Above the Storm*, the woman stopped Jennita.

"I've been wanting to get closer to God," she said. "I have a friend who always tells me about his experience with God—how he prays and sees answers. But I just can't seem to do that. God seems too busy or far away to hear about all of my problems. But I think this book will help me!"

"Yes, I think it will too!" Jennita said, turning to a specific page. "Let me read this little section to you," she said, sharing one of her favorite passages on prayer.

Seeming touched, the woman began to share. "You know, I was raised Catholic, but I just never felt close to God. I know God exists, because He spared my life years ago when a serious virus attacked my heart. After that, I was in a wheelchair for years, but now I've even begun to walk again. I know God is real and that I have many reasons to be thankful to Him."

Jennita nodded. "Are there any specific requests you have for God? May I pray with you now?" she asked.

The woman eagerly agreed, and the pair bowed their heads. As Jennita prayed for her, the woman began to pray along, interjecting with various requests. After prayer, the woman eagerly signed up for Bible studies with the local Bible worker.

As Jennita closed the door behind her, her bag of books was a bit lighter. She had left behind *The Great Controversy* and *Peace Above the Storm*. Praise God that He is not too far away to hear the prayers of those who seek Him!

A messenger of hope

It was the last Sunday of the summer program, and Moses Ntekereze was really discouraged. He was ready to tell his leader, Lily Zhang, that he was done for the day. After all, people weren't that interested in what he had to offer.

While he was dealing with discouragement, a mother living in the neighborhood where Moses was working was disheartened. She had just finished having a conversation with her son. He was asking many questions about God and religion for which she didn't have satisfactory answers. Her son concluded that Christianity doesn't make sense, and so he would become an atheist. The mother was ready to walk out of the house, feeling like a total loser.

Then she whispered a prayer, "God, would you please send someone to my door with Christian books that will answer my son's questions?" She picked up a checkbook and wrote a check for $150, and on the memo line she marked it, "Christian books."

Twenty minutes later, Moses came to her door with Christian books! He met both the woman and her son—who pummeled him with question after question about Christianity. It was obvious to Moses that God had begun to take over his canvass. "Every time he asked me a question," Moses shared later, "I pulled out a book and showed how it would help answer his questions." God showed Moses exactly which book would answer each question!

At the end, what a sight it was for him to see a stack of ten books on the coffee table and a check in his hand, money prayerfully designated for Christian literature. What an encouragement it was for him to know that he was God's messenger that day, a messenger of hope.

2
God's Providence

"From one man he made all the nations . . . he marked out their appointed times in history and the boundaries of their lands. God did this so that they would seek him and perhaps reach out for him and find him, though he is not far from any one of us" (Acts 17:26, 27, NIV).

When persecution arose against the early Christians in Jerusalem, they were scattered abroad and "went everywhere preaching the word" (Acts 8:4). It was at this time that Philip the evangelist, one of the first deacons, was directed by an angel to take the road from Jerusalem to Gaza, without any further instruction. As he was traveling that road, he came upon a servant of the Queen of Ethiopia, "a eunuch of great authority" (v. 27), who was studying the scroll of the prophet Isaiah. The Spirit of God then gave a specific command to Philip to "go near and overtake this chariot" (v. 29). Philip immediately responded, having to run to catch the chariot. Upon reaching the man, Philip was able to preach Christ to him and baptize him. Immediately after the baptism, "the Spirit of the

Lord caught Philip away" (v. 39) to preach again at Azotus and the regions beyond.

The Lord was accomplishing an important purpose through this divine appointment. "This Ethiopian was a man of good standing and of wide influence. God saw that when converted he would give others the light he had received and would exert a strong influence in favor of the gospel" (*The Acts of the Apostles,* 107).

In His providence God still arranges divine appointments for the furtherance of the gospel. He orchestrates meetings between His servants and His lost sheep, in order that they may find their way home and that they, too, become workers for Him.

Just as I am

Standing in the foyer of a Seventh-day Adventist church and looking up at a picture of Jesus, Moises Garcia spoke to Ricky Camacho: "You know, I wasn't going to come to church today, but I read last night in the book that I bought from you that I can come to God just as I am. That's the only reason I came. I never knew before that I could."

Just days earlier, Ricky and his student Karen Yanez met Moises at his home. At the time, nothing about the experience seemed noteworthy. Moises bought four books and asked what church they attended. When they told him, he politely asked for the address as well. They gave it to him and said their goodbyes.

The following Sabbath, Moises walked into the local Adventist church and told Ricky why he had come. Ricky sat with Moises during potluck and discovered that there was more to this quiet man's story. Three years earlier, when Moises lived in a different state, a literature evangelist had sold him a *Bible Readings for the Home.* He read the book and learned about the Sabbath. When he told his parents, they told him he was crazy. His pastor told him, "You can believe that if you want to, but don't tell anyone else about it." Moises chose to believe in spite of the criticism. But it wasn't until he read *Steps to Christ* that he realized something essential about God's character: God accepts us just as we are.

After attending church that first Sabbath, Moises met the local pastor and began Bible studies. It wasn't long before he was baptized. Today, he is an active member, and he and Ricky are good friends. Recently he told Ricky, "Thank you so much for the work you do as a literature evangelist."

There are millions of people with false ideas about God's character, and many people feel that God could never accept them or forgive their sins. The world needs more Christians who are willing to share the truth about His character! God is not an exacting judge, waiting to punish sinners. Instead, He graciously accepts us just as we are and transforms us into His image. After all, as the Psalmist asked, "who could stand" if God kept track of our iniquities? "But there is forgiveness with You, that You may be feared" (Psalm 130:3, 4).

The son's interest

The garage door was open, and a few people covered in tattoos had gathered together to have a good time. Cases of beer littered the driveway, and cigarette smoke filled the air. Donna Coon, afraid to approach the party scene, reminded herself of the morning's worship thought that angels were with her.

"What are you selling?" one of the group asked.

"We're not interested, whatever it is!" another called out.

Donna persisted in spite of the laughter of most of the group. She noticed, however, there was one woman who remained quiet. Finally, Donna left, unsuccessful.

Two doors down, a boy in his teens answered. While he wasn't interested in any books, he noticed that she also carried a DVD and asked about it. Donna showed him the *Final Events* DVD. The boy explained to Donna that he had gone with his mother to many different churches, but that they all pushed religion without explaining the Bible. He had pretty much given up on religion; however, the interest was still in the back of his mind, and he was especially intrigued by the book of Revelation. The boy went back into the house to find money for the DVD but returned unsuccessful.

"My mom is just a couple doors down, in the neighbor's garage," he told Donna. "Will you go ask my mom to get this DVD for me?"

Donna's heart sank, but she decided she had to try. She turned and headed back to the garage where she'd been ridiculed.

"Excuse me, but which one of you lives at that house?" she asked the group, pointing to the teenager's house. "Your son wanted me to ask you something."

The woman who had remained quiet before spoke up. "That's my house."

Donna quickly explained what the boy had told her.

"He said he was interested?" the woman asked in surprise. "I would do anything to help my son be guided toward God. I just know I can't show him myself."

Donna shared the *Final Events* DVD with her, as well as *God's Answers to Your Questions*. "This book can help answer any questions your son might have as he learns about the Bible on his own," she told the woman.

As she got together the funds for the material, the woman began to cry. "Three years ago today my husband left us. We've felt lost ever since then."

There in front of the entire group, Donna prayed for the hurting woman, and the woman apologized for how Donna had been treated when she first came by. As Donna left, the garage full of people was silent.

In His famous mountaintop sermon, Jesus said, "Blessed are you when they revile and persecute you, and say all kinds of evil against you falsely for My sake. Rejoice and be exceedingly glad, for great is your reward in heaven, for so they persecuted the prophets who were before you" (Matthew 5:11, 12). Donna, though ridiculed at first, is now hoping that part of her heavenly reward will be seeing mother and son saved. She writes, "Just as this lady wanted to do anything to help her son find hope, so our heavenly Father continues to do anything to open the hearts of those willing to get to know Him. I pray that someday soon I will see both mother and son in heaven."

Vessels of mercy

As Jennita Schmidt approached a small dry-cleaning business, she noticed the line of customers inside. Feeling the gentle nudge of the Holy Spirit not to enter quite yet, she decided to talk to the few people she saw in the parking lot. About ten minutes later, she returned to the business, just as the last customer was leaving.

"What are you selling?" the owner asked, by way of greeting. "I am busy, and I have no money . . . but wait a minute, and I will talk to you." Jennita sat down to wait.

After a few minutes, the owner emerged from the back of the store and indicated that he was ready to listen. Jennita introduced herself and handed the man a health book called *Foods That Heal*. As the man opened it, the book fell open to a spread about heart-healthy foods, and Jennita pointed it out.

"How did you know I have heart problems?" the man exclaimed.

"I didn't!" Jennita responded. "The book just fell open to that page, so I emphasized it."

"Well, it couldn't be coincidence!" the man argued.

"Sir, I believe you're right. I really believe that there is someone who knows just what you need," Jennita responded, handing him *Peace Above the Storm*.

The man read the front cover aloud. "'Peace Above the Storm: Freedom from worry, guilt, and fear.' Freedom from worry—you have no idea how worried I am about my family and my son! 'Guilt'—I do feel a bit guilty. No, I feel really guilty, and I regret so many things. I don't think I'll ever be able to make it right. 'And fear'—I am afraid that fear almost controls my life!"

Jennita flipped the pages of the book until she found a specific quotation. She read, " 'Keep your wants, your joys, your sorrows, your cares, and your fears before God.' "

"May I read this out loud?" the man asked. When Jennita nodded, he read the quotation, stopping at each sentence to explain how it applied to his current situation. "I am a very busy man," he told her. "But I am taking time to talk to you because I know this is important. When I see young people like you who are doing something worthwhile, it gives me hope for my family. My business is not going well, and this is a bad time, but I will help you out."

Jennita then pulled out *The Great Controversy*. The business owner stared at the flag pictured on the cover for a moment before speaking.

"Do you see that flag out there in the parking lot?" he asked. "I see that flag every day, and I wonder how long our country will be free. Why is God no longer the center of our country?"

A few minutes later, Jennita left the dry cleaner's, her bag four books lighter than before. She was sure that she had just met one of God's "vessels of mercy"—an individual God has "prepared beforehand for glory" (Romans 9:23).

Stolen opportunity

A student literature evangelist's day starts early, with breakfast and worship as a team. One morning, Janine Kowell decided to call home in the few minutes between breakfast and worship. She set her purse next to the phone in the office of the church where they were staying for the summer, and then she remembered she'd left her Bible at the breakfast table.

Thinking that no one would ever steal something in a church, she quickly ran back to the fellowship hall to collect her Bible. When she returned to the church office just moments later, her purse was gone. To her dismay, she found a trail of her belongings on the sidewalk outside. Following the trail, she was able to collect most of her belongings, including the purse itself, but her cash and bankcards were gone.

Janine missed worship that morning while she canceled her debit card and filled out a long police report. Afterward, she wanted nothing more than to take the day off and have a pity party. Her leader, while understanding and helpful, had a different idea.

"Janine, God just may have a divine appointment for you today that Satan is trying to steal from you. This may be the very day that God is calling you to trust in Him through the trials and persevere all the more," he said, encouraging her.

Janine's heart sank, but she knew he might be right. After taking a few minutes to pray over the matter, she knew she needed to go out in faith, regardless of how she felt.

However, by early evening, hardly anyone had accepted her books, and the discouraging thoughts returned. As the evening wore on, Janine was beginning to feel sorry for herself and was tempted to quit a few minutes early. Instead, she tried to silence the selfish thoughts. She reminded herself that these temptations were from the enemy, that God had called her to share His words of life with others, and so she kept going.

Just before the evening ended, Janine recalled an incident from earlier that afternoon. A man had answered his door while on a phone call. He wasn't particularly interested in her books but gave her a dollar for the pamphlet version of *Steps to Christ*. As she was leaving, he called after her, "Hey, my roommate really likes to cook. If you come back, he'll probably get your cookbook!"

As dusk now approached, Janine remembered the man's comment and wondered if she should go back. She knew that when people said, "Come back later," it was usually just an excuse. "Come back later and talk to my roommate" seemed even more unlikely to bring any results. Nevertheless, she decided to try.

Turning the corner, Janine saw the man she'd met previously pulling out of his driveway, with another man sitting next to him in the passenger seat. Figuring that the other man was the roommate, she flagged them down.

Addressing the man in the passenger seat, Janine said, "I heard you like to cook, and I thought you might be interested in this cookbook."

The roommate looked bewildered, but a look of amazement flooded over the face of the man she'd met that afternoon.

"I know you actually came back for me," he cut in. "I read that little book cover to cover. I was so impacted that I called my girlfriend and started reading it to her. My parents raised me going to church, but it's been a long time since I've gone. Recently, though, I've been thinking I need to get back to church. After reading this little book, I see what I really need is to find Jesus for myself."

Before her leader returned to pick her up for the night, Janine left Richard with several Bible studies on getting to know Jesus. She prayed with him and collected his contact information. A local Bible worker began studying the Bible with Richard and his girlfriend, and about a year later, both got baptized.

In thinking back on her experience, Janine writes, "Divine appointments can and do happen when we continue to trust in God despite our difficulties and discouragements!" The Psalmist puts it this way: "Be of good courage, and He shall strengthen your heart, all you who hope in the LORD" (Psalm 31:24).

Books about the Lord

"I don't really have money right now," the slightly plump woman told Jensen Ruud, after he'd shown her three different books. "But my sister is inside. Let me go talk to her. Why don't you take a seat there, on the bench?" Returning Jensen's books to him, the woman disappeared into the house.

Jensen sat down to wait. One minute passed, then another, and another. As he continued to wait, Jensen began to pray. "Lord, if it is Your will, please bring the sister outside to see these books of truth. But if You want me to move on, then please let me know."

A few moments later, a tall, slender woman stepped out onto the porch. "I hear you have books about the Lord," she exclaimed with a big smile on her face. Jensen quietly thanked God for the opportunity to share. As the second sister took a seat next to Jensen, the first sister joined them on the porch. While she'd been the picture of apathy just minutes before, she suddenly seemed interested.

Jensen began to show the two women his books. *God's Answers to Your Questions* quickly became their favorite. One sister flipped through its pages to look at the different topics, then handed it to the other sister. "I want this one," one said, only to be followed by an objection from the other sister: "But that's the one I want!"

Jensen assured the sisters that they could both get a copy and radioed his leader for an extra copy. Eventually, the first sister selected two books and the second sister chose four. As the three shared their testimonies, one of the sisters said, "We don't even live here! We're from Georgia. Our family lives in this house, but they're gone right now."

Before he left, Jensen prayed, thanking God that He had brought them together at just the right time and asking that He would lead each of them closer to Jesus. As he left the house, Jensen was amazed at how God had directed their paths so that earnest seekers could receive truth. The words of Solomon to his son are also the words of God to each truth-seeker: "I have taught you in the way of wisdom; I have led you in right paths" (Proverbs 4:11).

Pressed down and running over

As David Young was working his way up one side of a street, he noticed a funeral home on the other side that was obviously hosting a memorial service. David realized that, since he was alone on the street, he would be responsible for visiting the funeral home. He did not relish the thought, but he kept sensing the urge that he must stop there. Relenting, he prayed, "OK, Lord. I'll give the grieving family a *Peace Above the Storm* if You provide the donation to cover it."

David continued making his way up the street. By the time he was ready to work back down the opposite side, he still had not received any extra donations. He began to think that he wouldn't have to stop at the funeral home after all!

At the last house before the funeral home, however, a kind older woman answered the door. She was interested in prophecy and gave David a large enough donation to cover all his prophecy material, as well as an additional book.

With the extra donation in hand, David remembered his commitment to God and headed to the funeral home. As he stepped inside, a woman greeted him.

"Will you please give this book to the family?" David asked, handing the woman *Peace Above the Storm*.

"Certainly. May I give you a donation for the book?" the woman responded quickly.

David was stunned. "Well, sure. Thank you!"

The woman found her purse and wrote a check for fifty dollars. Upon seeing the amount, David reached in his bag for a few additional books to leave for the family. When he handed the woman a copy of *Man of Peace*, she pulled him to a private corner.

"Are you a Seventh-day Adventist?" she asked.

"Yes, I am," David answered.

"I've been attending an Adventist church for some time, but I haven't been sure whether I should join or not. I've been praying about it. Meeting you today seems like an answer to my prayer!"

David discovered that day the rewards of generosity. When, in spite of his discomfort, he reached out to bless someone else, God richly repaid him—not only in extra donations but with an experience that allowed him to see God's omnipotence in action.

"God sent you here"

As Titus Morris made his way down a street, it seemed that every person he met had the same response: the door would open just long enough for the person inside to give a quick "I'm not interested," and then it would close again.

Keeping up a quick pace between the doors, Titus began to pray. "Lord, please use me to encourage someone! Let someone see the truth in these books. Please use these books to set someone free."

Soon, Titus met a woman named Rachel. Though her manner was very formal and business-like, she was willing to look at Titus's material. Titus handed her a *Peace Above the Storm*.

Looking down at the book's cover, Rachel sighed. "I found out just yesterday that my husband of seven years is cheating on me," she confessed. Even behind her business-like mask, Titus could see the deep pain in her eyes.

"I'm so sorry," Titus said, reaching out to turn the pages of the book Rachel held. "Let me show you something." Turning to the beginning of each chapter, Titus showed Rachel how each chapter had worked together to help him know God as a friend. As he talked, Rachel's formal demeanor began to relax.

"What's amazing is that God is so unlike the other people in our lives," Titus explained. "He's a friend who will never leave us, and He never lets us down."

Rachel nodded. "This is exactly what I need right now!" she exclaimed.

Rachel selected both *Peace Above the Storm* and *He Taught Love*. As Titus prayed for her, her eyes filled with tears.

"Thank you so much for coming, Titus! You can't know how much this means to me," Rachel said, giving Titus a grateful hug. "I'm sure God sent you here."

As he left Rachel's doorstep, Titus was also certain that God had sent him. He felt a deep gratitude to God for using him to answer Rachel's need—and his own prayer as well.

The voice at the truck stop

On a winter evening in 2008, the world economy was struggling, and so was Ron Park. He had spent nearly the entire day working at a truck stop, talking to the truck drivers on their mandatory driving breaks. All day long he had prayed with the drivers, but no one had wanted or been able to afford his books. The evening was cold and dark, and Ron wanted to go home. As Ron eyed the last truck in the lot that he'd not yet visited, he felt sure he heard a voice: "Go and knock on that truck's door."

Ron obeyed. Victor Lima opened the truck's door, and Ron began to show him his books.

"Are you a Seventh-day Adventist?" Victor asked, interrupting.

"Yes," Ron answered, surprised.

"I used to be a very active Adventist, when I lived in my country. But when I moved here, everything changed." Victor explained how he had started to pull away from God after his move, and that he had lived a faithless life in the many years since. Recently, however, he'd started to miss his love for God. He wanted to return to church, but he was sure he'd drifted too far from God to go back. So, Victor had begun to pray—"Lord, if you want me to come back, please show me a sign."

"And I think you are God's answer to my prayer!" Victor finished.

Before they parted ways, Victor chose three of Ron's religious books, they prayed together, and Ron collected Victor's contact information.

Months later, Ron wondered what had become of Victor and gave him a call. Victor told him that he had returned to church, and he was very happy to be back in

God's arms again.

Ron often considers what might have happened if he'd given in to discouragement and headed home before finishing. "I'm sure God would have done something else to save Victor," he says, "but I'm so glad I obeyed God's voice that night. I had the privilege of being God's instrument to rescue a lost soul!"

Romans 6:13 explains that each of us are to be God's "instruments of righteousness." Will you also obey His voice? The privilege will be unforgettable.

Prepared in advance

"What church are you from?" the home-health assistant asked Rachel Moravetz.

"We're working with the company that puts out the blue Bible story books," Rachel started to say.

"Yes, but what church are you from?" the woman, Maggie, repeated her question.

"I'm a Seventh-day Adventist Christian," Rachel said.

"Ah. I've been watching 3ABN recently," Maggie explained. "Come on in!"

Rachel stepped inside the home where Maggie was working, providing health-care to an older couple. As they visited, Rachel discovered that Maggie was already convinced of the Adventist message about the state of the dead and hell.

"You must show me everything you have!" Maggie instructed Rachel.

Happily, Rachel complied. Maggie was especially interested in the *Final Events* DVD she'd seen advertised on 3ABN. When she saw *The Great Controversy*, she read each chapter heading and decided she would probably agree with each one. As Rachel handed her the last book, Maggie sat back, a little stunned.

"Maggie," she said to herself out loud, "you know you've been thinking about this!" Turning to Rachel, she explained, "God has been impressing me for a few months now that these messages were important and that I needed to study them more." With that, Maggie chose six items, including *Final Events* and *The Great Controversy*. She also agreed to personal Bible studies.

As she left, Rachel was amazed at the evidence of God working ahead of her. When God gave His moral and ceremonial laws to Moses to relay to the Israelites, He included a promise that applies to Christian workers today: "Behold, I send an Angel before you to keep you in the way and to bring you into the place which I have prepared" (Exodus 23:20). In Maggie's case, God had been preparing months in advance!

Uphold the fallen

While attempting to answer Lorenzo Rolle's knock on her door, an elderly woman fell and hit her head. Obviously in pain, she called out to Lorenzo and his student that she was not interested. Through the screen door, Lorenzo could see that she was having difficulty getting up. She rolled to the right, and when that failed, she rolled to the left. Lorenzo wanted to help, but the screen door was locked, and there was no one else at home to call for help. Finally, the woman told them where to find the key.

Praying that God would help him locate the key quickly, Lorenzo dropped to the ground to look underneath the steps. Finding the key, he let himself and his student in the house.

As Lorenzo helped the woman up off the floor and into her chair, the woman's dog urinated on the floor. The student quickly cleaned up the mess. Then they helped the woman get a glass of water to take her medication.

By the time they had finished helping her, the woman's attitude had changed. They prayed together, and the woman decided to keep two of their books: *Peace Above the Storm* and *The Great Controversy*.

As Lorenzo reflected on the experience, he realized it was a parable of how God works with each of us. He had to pick the woman up from her fall, and God promises to "[uphold] all who fall, and raise up all who are bowed down" (Psalm 145:14). His student cleaned up the dog's mess on the floor, and God certainly "[cleanses] us from all unrighteousness" (1 John 1:9). Finally, even though they were strangers, the woman was willing to let them in when she realized she needed their help. The book of Revelation pictures Jesus standing by the door of our hearts and knocking. If you don't know Him yet, but realize you need help, won't you ask Him in?

3

The Great Controversy

"We can do nothing against the truth,
but for the truth" (2 Corinthians 13:8).

W hile the apostle Paul was imprisoned at Rome, he wrote his letter to the Philippian church to calm some of their anxieties about his circumstances. As he shared some experiences, he told them of how some of his enemies would repeat his teachings to stir up strife, hoping to bring a heavier punishment upon him. Yet, as a result, he said, it "actually turned out for the furtherance of the gospel . . . to the whole palace guard, and to all the rest" (Phil. 1:12, 13). The same apostle wrote to the believers in Corinth that we can "do nothing against the truth, but for the truth" (2 Corinthians 13:8). In other words, it is God's truth, and no weapon formed against it will prosper. No matter how hard the enemy resists it, the truth of God will prevail.

The same is still true today. The message of "present truth" is presented in the book *The Great Controversy*. The powers of heaven are laboring earnestly through consecrated workers to get this book into the hands of people everywhere because it "contain[s] truth for this time,—truth that is to be proclaimed in all parts of the world." "The book *The Great Controversy*, I appreciate above silver or gold, and I greatly desire that it shall come before the people" (*Colporteur Ministry, 124, 128*).

This book has been the means of converting unnumbered souls to Christ and His Word, me being one of them. There are many, many more to come. Let us, then, delay no longer in cooperating with the armies of heaven for the widespread distribution of this book. This work will go forward. God's truth will at last be victorious.

The book that wouldn't burn

The student literature evangelist walked over to the waiting van. "You will never believe what just happened!" The student had handed *The Great Controversy* to a woman at the door and had begun to share the canvass. The woman took the book in her hands and looked at the cover while the student shared her opening line. At that very moment her face lit up with a bright smile, and she started shouting, "That's the book! That's the book!"

Stunned, the student had stopped canvassing, and the woman shared her story.

The year before, the woman had obtained *The Great Controversy* from a student. As she began to read the book, she realized that Jesus was coming soon and decided to commit her life to Him.

As she drew closer to God, however, she had a nagging question that haunted her. Why did God allow her husband to continue beating and abusing her? How could He let that happen to someone who wanted to live for Him?

She ruminated over this question incessantly, until finally it occurred to her that just as God had changed her life, He could change her husband's also. After all, He was God!

She then began to leave the book on the coffee table every day, hoping her husband would read it. For weeks she left it there, but nothing happened.

One day she came home from the grocery store and found her husband sitting in a chair, crying! He was reading *The Great Controversy*! He looked up at her and said, "You'll never believe what just happened."

He had picked up the book from the coffee table and begun to read it. But the more he read, the angrier he got! He was a devout Catholic and took immediate offense to the accounts of Catholic history.

He got so angry that he took the book and threw it into the fire burning in the fireplace.

Then he looked at the fire. He couldn't believe it. The book was not burning! He pulled the book from the fire with a pair of tongs. He said to himself, "This book must be from God!"

Like King Nebuchadnezzar of old, the man saw that fire has no power over anything God does not permit to burn. He began to read the book, and eventually he, too, gave his life to God.

The stunned student was speechless as she listened to the woman's story. That book that she carried in her bag was powerful! It had refused to burn! And it had transformed a family in less than one year!

Not by might nor by power

"Today is GC day!" Heidi Hunt's leader announced as the team drove to their territory for the day. "Let's be praying for *Great Controversy* experiences all day today."

A few minutes later, Heidi and her partner were dropped off on a street of businesses. As Heidi stepped from the van, the first business loomed in front of her. It was a huge, school-like building. She felt her courage waning as she looked at the imposing structure. After praying with her partner for *Great Controversy* experiences, Heidi made her way toward the giant building, her courage continuing to melt away.

The main entrance opened into a large open space. Directly in front of her was an exercise room surrounded by glass windows. To either side of the exercise room, two wide halls opened up. For a moment she stood still, watching the people lifting weights and running on treadmills. She felt lost and confused. What kind of business was this? It seemed like a cross between a school and a fitness center. And, more important, where should she start?

Heidi knew that she needed to act confident, as if she knew exactly where she was going. Doing so would help her avoid suspicion, giving her opportunity to talk to as many people as possible. But her feelings ran contrary to her knowledge—she felt like disappearing and finding an easier place to meet people! "God, please help me know what to do," she prayed silently.

Heidi walked around the corner and spotted a sign for a restroom down one of the hallways. Knowing she needed a little extra wisdom from God, she locked herself in a bathroom stall and prayed earnestly. "Lord, please help me to know who to talk to! Help me to meet the people I need to meet before I get asked to leave." As she prayed for courage and divine appointments in the large building, her spirits lifted, and she felt God's courage in her heart.

When Heidi left the restroom and headed down the hall, she met a man who looked as though he worked there. She showed him her books, and he made a donation for a *Peace Above the Storm*. Feeling encouraged, she walked on past a row of small offices filled with student workers. She stepped inside, approached a young man, and began to offer her materials.

The young man showed interest in *The Great Controversy*, but when Heidi explained how he could make a donation, he made an excuse. "Oh, I don't have money," he told Heidi.

Heidi persisted, letting him know that she could accept a credit card if neces-sary. After several attempts, Heidi could see that her persistence was of no use, and she left the office saddened. She spent the next few minutes meeting as many people in the strange building as she could, and eventually she was ready to move on to another business.

Instead of using the exit closest to her, Heidi retraced her steps to the same door she had entered. Pausing to reflect, she realized that the other exit was not only closer but also would have led most directly to the next business. Though she didn't know it at the time, she later realized that the Holy Spirit must have been guiding her steps to the other door!

As she crossed the parking lot to the next business, she heard someone calling her. Turning, she saw the young man she had tried to convince to get *The Great Controversy*.

"Heidi! After you left, I kept being bothered by the idea that I should have gotten that book. I've been waiting and watching the window to see if you'd come back. When I saw you walk by just now, I knew I had to come after you," the young man explained. He happily pulled out his credit card to offer a donation for the precious book.

As they parted ways, Heidi rejoiced in how God had answered her prayers. She'd experienced a *Great Controversy* divine appointment in her very first business of the day. In addition, God had given her much-needed courage, sent the Holy Spirit to convict the young man's heart, and guided her steps so that she would return the way she had come.

"I am reminded of a special promise as I reminisce about this experience," Heidi wrote later. " ' "Not by might nor by power, but by My Spirit," says the Lord of hosts' " (Zechariah 4:6). May we daily surrender to His will and place our hand of weakness into His hand of strength so we can experience more of His Spirit!"

Undercover Christian

It was a cold and clear evening. I (Kamil Metz) had dropped Shahin Daniel off in a normal middle-class neighborhood.

As Shahin knocked on a door, it was answered by a teenage girl and her younger brother. He soon learned that they were a Muslim family from Pakistan. His heart went out to them. He himself had once been a Muslim, so he prayed that God would give him the right words to minister to them. They told him that their parents were not home, so he began to show the teenage girl the books, beginning with one in particular—*The Great Controversy*.

At that moment the Muslim young woman motioned for her little brother to leave. Shahin thought to himself, *She doesn't want her little brother to hear anything about Jesus. She's trying to "protect" him.* Boy, was he wrong.

The situation was this: she simply had a dearly cherished secret that she wanted to share. When her little brother was well into the house, she whispered, "I am a Christian too."

Having a similar ethnic background, Shahin knew what that meant, and his heart went out to her. If her parents discovered her conversion to Christianity, she could be killed.

He told her that she needed to read *The Great Controversy* and that he would leave it with her for any donation. At that moment her brother appeared at the door, having secretly listened to their conversation, unbeknownst to them, and he said, "I have five dollars!" He ran inside, quickly retrieved it, and handed it over.

Shahin gave them the precious cargo of truth and left, but his prayer for them has remained that will God bless them and keep them faithful to Him!

A friendly recommendation

As Keri Scau approached a woman watering her yard, she had the impression that she should not begin this interaction in her normal fashion. When meeting a woman, Keri usually began by showing a cookbook or a book of children's stories. This time, however, she reached for *The Great Controversy*.

Even so, the woman lifted her hand in protest. "I do not need another book!" she exclaimed. "I have *heaps* of books!" Motioning with her hand, she led Keri around to the back of the house. Entering, Keri could see that the woman was not exaggerating. She truly had heaps of books—and nearly every one was about Christianity, history, or economics.

"If these are the kinds of books you like, you just have to take a look at this one!" Keri insisted. "You will love it."

Eventually the woman was won over and agreed to add *The Great Controversy* to her impressive collection. Keri left, sending up a silent prayer that the woman would read the book instead of just adding it to the piles on the shelves. As she whispered, "Amen," she heard the woman's voice calling after her.

"Hey, come back!"

Surprised, Keri returned to the yard to find the woman, telephone in hand.

"What's your name? I'm calling my friend down the street to tell her you're coming. She likes to read like I do—and she has money!"

Keri left the yard a second time, feeling reassured that the woman was likely to read a book she was willing to recommend. Finding the house with the brick perimeter walls she'd been told about, she knocked and asked for Terry. A few minutes later, Keri was back on the front porch with a nearly empty bag and a large check in hand. Terry did indeed like to read, and, encouraged by her friend's recommendation, she had wanted every single religious book Keri carried—including *The Great Controversy*!

Solomon wrote that "he who walks with wise men will be wise" (Proverbs 13:20). What kinds of recommendations do you find yourself giving to your friends?

A day of miracles

During the summer of 1995, leader Eugene Prewitt was working for the day with his student, Ester Ramdin. They were making appointments to show their larger sets of hardcover books and leaving behind their smaller paperbacks for donations. One of the first people they encountered tried to tell them about a comet that was obscuring a spaceship. They listened a bit and then left them with *The Great Controversy*.

Just a few houses later, a man told them he would buy their book if they would buy his house. They couldn't do that, of course, but the man still ended up getting *The Great Controversy*.

Later, another man invited the two students in. He began to weep and shared how his children had grown up and gone astray. Seeing Eugene and Ester reminded him of what he wished for his children. He bought four of their books (including *The Great Controversy*) and asked the students to pray for his children. They did.

Just a hundred yards from that home, the pair met a nice woman. She also took *The Great Controversy* and told them that they ought to visit her father. She pointed to the home where they had just been. Already God was answering the father's prayers!

Down the road, as Eugene and Ester approached a home, they could hear the voice of Alexander Scourby. They knew that meant someone was listening to the Bible on tape, and they were excited to see what God had in store. But the man at the door was unkind and sent them away.

Around a bend or two, the pair came to a home where a family reunion was happening. People were milling around outside. Who should they approach? They picked one friendly-looking face, and the woman was interested. But she asked if they could follow her to her home so she could get her money. The two literature evangelists agreed. They followed her car and, to their dismay, the woman pulled into the home where the Bible on tape was being read! They sat in their car and prayed nervously as she entered the home where they'd been rebuffed just moments earlier. The woman emerged with her purse, paid for the books, and the two of them left right away!

Later the pair came to a trailer where they met a man who wanted them to watch a video about black helicopters. He showed them his gun and shared some conspiracy theories. Eugene and Ester listened. And then they sold him a *Great Controversy*. He asked the two what church they were with, and they told him. He said that he had a friend who had once been an Adventist. They asked how to get to that man's home.

On their way to the ex-Adventist's home, they prayed. The sun was going down. They had only one copy of *The Great Controversy* book left. They knocked at the door, and a woman answered. She didn't seem to recognize the book, but they sold it to her. For a moment, the pair paused, praising God silently. All six of their *Great Controversy* books were now in people's homes! Then they asked the woman if her husband was around. She said he was down the hill giving a Bible Study.

So Eugene and Ester went down the hill. They met the husband and a young couple. They showed the young couple the covers of the Conflict of the Ages series and told them about the books.

"Can you come back later?" the couple asked. Knowing that wasn't likely to work out for the couple's best interest, Eugene and Ester pressed for a quicker decision. The couple agreed to talk and pray about it between themselves while the students waited in the car. Ten minutes later, as the couple invited them back in, the ex-Adventist walked out—refusing to meet the students' eyes.

"Are these books by a prophet?" the couple asked.

Suspecting that the ex-Adventist had made some uncomplimentary remarks about Ellen White, Eugene asked the couple to open their Bibles. Opening his Bible to Ephesians 4, Eugene gave the couple a Bible study on spiritual gifts. At the end of the study, the couple ordered a large, hardcover set of the Conflict of the Ages set—which includes *The Great Controversy*!

"Who is so great a God as our God?" Asaph asked in a psalm. "You are the God who does wonders" (Psalm 77:13, 14). Eugene later echoed that sentiment, remarking, "It was a day of miracles!"

Is canvassing even my "gift"?

"Why am I doing this?" The question persistently went through Taylor Hinkle's mind as he went door to door. He had been canvassing for a few weeks now and wondered how effective he really was at it. Understanding that God gives different gifts to different people, he concluded that canvassing wasn't his "gift." Maybe he could use his gifts in a more effective way.

The next morning before the canvassing team went out, Taylor prayed for God to make it clear if He really wanted him to continue canvassing. The students loaded into the vans, and they were off. During the entire ride to their territory, Taylor was praying in his heart for God to make it clear if He wanted him to continue. After

46

what seemed like an eternity, he was dropped off to canvass.

Before he even knocked on the first door, he prayed again that God would make it clear whether he should continue in the canvassing ministry that summer.

As Taylor worked his way down the street, some people got a few books, but still nothing out of the ordinary really spoke to him.

Then Taylor knocked on a door and Emily answered.

Handing her a cookbook, Taylor said, "*Seven Secrets* offers you the latest information on healthful cooking. It helps people to lose weight, lower cholesterol, and reverse diabetes."

Emily didn't say anything.

Wanting to find something to talk about, Taylor asked, "What church do you go to?"

The silence continued for a moment, but then Emily teared up suddenly and let out, "You are going to make me cry. You see, I am overweight, my husband has terribly high blood pressure, and my father-in-law has diabetes. Then you start asking me about God. I have been struggling to know if God is really there. Does He exist? Does He care?" She had begun to cry.

"Every time I look at the trees and see different things in creation, I can't help but think God must exist, but if he does, why is it that He doesn't help me? Does He care for me?

"I began to pray recently that if God really existed that He would make it clear," she continued, "and here you are standing at my door!"

"I believe that God has sent me here to your house today to show you how much He cares for you," Taylor replied.

Taylor handed Emily *The Great Controversy*.

"This book answers questions like, 'Why, if God is so good, is this world so bad? Why is it that bad things happen to good people?' It helps us see that the suffering we face is not an isolated issue, but there is something much bigger happening behind the scenes. Satan is doing all he can to make the lives of men and women miserable and then make it look as though God is responsible for their misery. But, Emily, God loves you. God wants you to know He cares about you, and that is why He has sent me here to your house this evening."

By this time she was just sobbing. "Praise God for sending you here this evening," she choked out.

Emily wanted to understand more about what Taylor was talking about, so she got *The Great Controversy* and *Man of Peace*.

"Is there anything I can use to teach my kids about God, as well?" Emily asked. Taylor showed her two children's Bible books, and she excitedly got them as well.

She signed up for personal Bible studies, and Taylor prayed with her before he left.

She went back into the house a different woman. She had peace. She now understood there is a God, and He cares for her.

How many Emilys are there in the world—people waiting to understand that there is a loving God in heaven who cares about their struggles in this world? Longing for the peace that only knowledge of God can give, they struggle alone. If only someone would go to them and share God's message with them. Is God calling you to go? Maybe your "Emily experience" will be the answer to your own prayer.

And what did Taylor learn about God's need of him in the canvassing work? Yes, he was needed! God could use him!

Note: canvassing is not one of the gifts of the Spirit! It is one of the ways in which young and old answer the gospel commission and say, "I will go!"

I believe in aliens

Christopher Da'Costa was working in a very interesting town that day. The whole community seemed very much into New Age, and it was difficult to make any direct connection with the Bible using his books.

On that particular day in that community, Christopher walked into an industrial business and presented his books to a manager. As he was sharing his books with Caley, the head manager of this prestigious business and school of insurance, she began to unravel her life story to him.

About five minutes into her story, Caley began to eloquently explain how she became, and why she still was, an atheist. She was raised as a Christian but converted to evolutionism at quite a young age. As Caley began to tell Christopher that she thought most Christians were uneducated and uninformed in the realm of science and astronomy, Christopher shared briefly that he had been an evolutionist while he served in the military for many years. She was a little intrigued at Christopher's testimony, but then, quite suddenly, the topic of conversation turned to aliens! She told him that she secretly believed in aliens.

"I definitely don't believe in the God of the Bible, but I do believe in higher powers of different sorts . . . like aliens!"

Caley, it turned out, believed aliens to be insightful creatures of information that visit the earth.

Christopher listened, paused for a moment after she had finished her thought, and then looked at her and said, in slow, measured tones, "I-am-an-alien." She looked at him in silence, incredulously at first, then her demeanor turned to great respect. "I have been sent from those above," he finished.

"Wait, you've been sent from the aliens?" she asked excitedly.

"I have been an alien in a strange land," he said, quoting Exodus 18:3 without saying the Bible reference.

Caley seemed overwhelmed. She couldn't believe what she was hearing! She was convinced that Christopher was either an alien or sent from the aliens. Christopher began to tell her how he and many of his friends were actually aliens, "strangers and pilgrims on the earth" (Hebrews 11:13, KJV).

With that, Caley unquestioningly responded, "If what you say is true, then I desperately want any information you have for me today."

"This book, *The Great Controversy*, is definitely a book of information you need if you would like to become as informed as real aliens on the earth," Christopher replied.

She grasped the book eagerly and began to open it. Seeing Bible verses, she questioned, "But it talks about the Bible?"

"Ma'am," Chris responded soberly, "this is what they said to share" (thinking of the Trinity).

She looked thoughtful for a moment and then relented, requesting two copies.

Are you letting God use you in all the right places and at any given moment? It was only God's orchestration for the young colporteur, a former evolutionist, to meet another searching evolutionist. Let God use you today, and remember you are an alien in this land!

Her two favorite things

While going door to door on a hot summer afternoon, Jensen Ruud met an elderly woman who immediately invited him inside. They had just begun to introduce themselves when Jensen noticed the large picture that hung behind her couch. It was a picture of the Ten Commandments.

"That's a really nice picture that you have there, ma'am. I like it a lot!" Jensen told the woman.

"Why, thank you!" she replied. "Let me show you something else that I really like."

She led Jensen to a shelf with a clear plastic cube. Inside the cube was a laser-etched image of the Statue of Liberty. She had recently visited New York and thoroughly enjoyed her visit. She informed Jensen that the Statue of Liberty was her favorite part of the trip.

This must be a divine appointment. I must show her this book! Jensen thought, fingering an edition of *The Great Controversy* with a rather unusual picture on its cover— the Statue of Liberty holding the Ten Commandments in her hands! The two sat down in the woman's living room, and Jensen began showing his books. His hopes were not disappointed.

"Oh! It has the Statue of Liberty and the Ten Commandments," the woman exclaimed as Jensen showed her *The Great Controversy*.

As they continued chatting, the woman's face grew very serious. "Now, I'm going to ask you a question that no one has ever been able to answer," she told Jensen with the utmost sincerity. "How did our churches today end up straying from the Bible?"

Instead of answering, Jensen directed her to the third chapter of *The Great Controversy*. This chapter clearly spells out how the early church lost its original faith. As they read the passage together, she gave an approving look.

"Yes, that's the answer I'd been looking for!" she said. She had done her own research and come to the very same conclusion. By the end of their visit, the woman made a donation for three books: *Peace Above the Storm*, *Man of Peace*, and *The Great Controversy*. Later, Jensen said, "I thank God for working so powerfully to put those books in her house, especially *The Great Controversy*! He used the very same symbols she loved, one fresh in her mind from her recent trip, and put just the right questions into her mind. There is no doubt that God wanted her to have that book at that exact time!"

Two people, one soul

For several years, Bamiji Ibironke had been working as a golf caddie in Detroit. Over the course of those years, he developed a burden for the souls of his co-workers.

As he began sharing the Bible with them, he noticed one of his friends in particular was becoming interested in spiritual things.

He continued to share with his friend the significance of the Bible, and, while doing so, recommended the book *The Great Controversy* as he continued to study.

At the peak of his interest, however, Bamiji felt called to go canvassing for the summer. He struggled with the call, wondering if it would be better to continue studying with the friend rather than canvass, but he listened to the voice of God and chose to canvass.

During the closing weeks of the program, one of Bamiji's friends, Sebastien, said that he canvassed someone who said he knew him! He explained that a young man opened the door and, after being canvassed on *The Great Controversy*, said that he would get it because one of his friends had previously told him about the book. Sebastien then asked him who his friend was, and he said, "Bamiji." It turned out to be Bamiji's very same friend and co-worker!

Bamiji thanked God for showing him that *He* was saving his friend, and that if you trust in God and give yourself fully to Him, He will give you the desire of your heart.

Psalm 37:4, 5 says, "Delight yourself also in the Lord, and He shall give you the desire of your heart. Commit your way to the Lord, trust also in Him, and He shall bring it to pass."

The stabbing pain

"Mobile one, this is Ellen. Ready for pick up!" the radio crackled as I (Kamil) was driving the canvassing van. Even over the radio, I could hear the urgency in Ellen Bascom's voice, so I quickly turned the van around to head toward the street she was canvassing. I found Ellen sitting on the curb, only halfway down the block I had given her to work.

"Jump in!" I called out of the window. *I wonder what could be wrong?* I thought to myself as Ellen made her way to the van.

"Kamil, I can't do this anymore!" Ellen said emphatically as she climbed into the front seat.

"Why? What's wrong?" I asked gently, thinking someone had been rude to her and hurt her feelings. A couple of Scripture promises popped into mind as I waited to hear what had happened.

"I mean, I can't canvass anymore! I've been having the weirdest experience ever! I just talked to a nice woman at her door. I showed her a cookbook, and everything was fine. But when I began to show her *The Great Controversy*, I got this intense pain in my stomach—like I was being stabbed! It was so bad, I could hardly talk!"

She described how she had gasped for air, alarming the woman at the door. Yet, somehow, breathless and feeling an intense pain in her stomach, she had managed to get through her presentation. The woman chose to get the book. And when she had at last given a donation for *The Great Controversy* and signed up for Bible studies, the pain had subsided immediately.

At the next door, the scenario repeated itself. The moment the woman at the door had *The Great Controversy* in her hands, Ellen was so overwhelmed with pain that she could barely speak! This second woman also took *The Great Controversy* and signed up for Bible studies, and just as before, the pain went away as soon as the donation had been received and the Bible study recorded. But twice was too much for Ellen, and she called me on the radio.

What should I say to her? I thought to myself after hearing Ellen's experience. *This is such a strange experience, and I've never heard of this happening before in this ministry! I haven't been trained with how to deal with this issue. Too bad Doug Batchelor or Mark Finley aren't here. They seem to have all the answers. I'm just a college kid.*

I recognized that this was a supernatural phenomenon, I but didn't know what to say. The devil was obviously trembling that *The Great Controversy* was going out, and he was trying to annoy one of God's student literature evangelists. Suddenly a quotation I once memorized from the book *Colporteur Ministry* came to mind. *That's it!* I thought to myself.

"Ellen," I said aloud, "there's a quotation that has the answer to your situation. I then recited this promise to Ellen: " 'No sooner is the name of Jesus mentioned in love and tenderness than angels of God draw near, to soften and subdue the heart' [*Colporteur Ministry*, 111]."

"I don't get it," Ellen said, shaking her head. "How will that help my problem?"

"When you show people *The Great Controversy*, you need to mention the name of Jesus in love and tenderness as soon as you can! Then angels of God will draw near, and the evil angels will have to flee," I responded.

They prayed together, claiming the promise in *Colporteur Ministry*. Then, agreeing to try again, Ellen hopped out of the van and headed to the next house.

When the front door opened, Ellen showed the cookbook first, as always. Then she pulled out *The Great Controversy*, and, sure enough, the stabbing pain in her stomach returned. She could *hardly* talk! She felt inwardly doubled over in pain.

Somehow she managed to share her canvass of the book, quickly adding in Jesus' name as she did so. And as soon as she did, the pain *immediately* went away.

And praise the Lord, it never returned!

4

He Answers

*"I have prayed for you,
that your faith should not fail" (Luke 22:32).*

"I guess all we can do now is pray." Far too often I have heard professed Christians utter these faithless words of last resort. And far too often I have said them myself. While it is true that when all else fails, we still can pray, we should never treat prayer as a last resort—as something that we might as well try because nothing else worked. It is the single most powerful thing a soul-winner can do.

It is in the context of praying for others that Jesus tells us, " 'Where two or three are gathered together in My name, I am there in the midst of them' " (Matthew 18:20). And Jesus Himself told Peter, " 'I have prayed for you, that your faith should not fail' " (Luke 22:32). If Jesus felt it was important to pray for the spiritual welfare of others, how much more should we?

God loves to hear and answer our prayers, especially when we pray for the salvation of souls. We are assured that "the children of God are not left alone and defenseless. Prayer moves the arm of Omnipotence" (*Christ's Object Lessons,* 172). The book of James tells us that "the effective, fervent prayer of a righteous man avails much" (James 5:16).

Yet we must not assume that God will work in our behalf without our asking. The Bible says, "You do not have because you do not ask" (James 4:3, NIV). When we pray for God's intervention in the lives of others, He promises to work in miraculous ways to reach hearts that could not be reached otherwise. Ellen White wrote, "It is a part of God's plan to grant us, in answer to the prayer of faith, that which He would not bestow did we not thus ask" (*The Great Controversy,* 525).

Then let us be sure to approach the throne of grace with full assurance of faith that God is ready to hear and answer our earnest prayers.

Three knocks and three visits

Shaka was sitting in his living room when suddenly he heard a faint knock on his door. Thinking that it was a salesman, he purposely ignored it and continued on with his business. The knock repeated, but this time it was much louder. Then came yet another knock on the door. This time Shaka answered the door with two thoughts rushing through his mind: this must either be the police or a very persistent salesman. As he opened the door, Shaka was prepared to deliver a rather harsh rejection to an annoying door-to-door salesman until he saw who stood there. Standing there on his doorstep was a young woman, Ashlee Bohlman. She was a student literature evangelist.

Shaka stared at her and listened patiently as she shared with him what she was doing. Not wanting to reject the young woman, he gave a donation for a *Final Events* DVD by Doug Batchelor. As she was about to leave, Ashlee asked if he would mind if she prayed with him. Shaka didn't mind, and as she prayed, Shaka was surprised and touched by the sweetness and simplicity of the prayer.

I want to learn to pray like that! Shaka thought to himself. So, when Ashlee offered to have someone come by and study the Bible with him, he agreed. The young woman left encouraged but little expecting what a blessing would come from her short visit.

Not too long afterward, the local Bible worker, Jeff Bentley, tried to follow up with Shaka and his wife, Stephanie. They put off the Bible study twice. Still, Jeff persisted, visiting the couple a third time.

The evening of the third scheduled visit, Stephanie told her husband, "You aren't putting him off again, and I'm not cancelling with him myself!" They finally had their first study on Daniel chapter two. Shaka loved the first study and, all week, could not stop thinking about what he had learned. Both Shaka and his wife soaked up the truth they were learning whenever Jeff came over for the Bible studies.

When they learned about the Sabbath truth and other important Bible topics, their first reaction was one of anger. They felt as though everyone else knew this truth but had hidden it from them all their lives. Eventually, both Shaka and Stephanie were baptized into the local Adventist church. Now their entire family is actively involved in their church. Shaka serves as the GLOW coordinator for his church, and Stephanie is actively involved with the children's ministry.

The Lord moves in mighty and powerful ways. This time He planted a seed of truth through a student literature evangelist who faithfully went into the field of the Lord, and He watered the seed through the persistence and diligence of a Bible worker. "Then He [Jesus] said to His disciples, 'The harvest truly is plentiful, but the laborers are few. Therefore pray the Lord of the harvest to send out laborers into His harvest' " (Matthew 9:37, 38). And if we pray for laborers, we might just find we are the first ones God calls!

A drink and a prayer

Gina Campos approached two women standing outside a home. As she canvassed them, one woman seemed interested in her books, while the other was a little rude and interrupted her presentation several times. The interested woman ended up choosing a book of children's stories called *Storytime*, and Gina continued to the next house.

As she headed across the lawn, Gina noticed that the woman who had been rude to her was following her! The woman stopped Gina, informing her that this was her house and she wasn't interested.

Gina nodded. "That's all right, ma'am. But may I have a drink of water, please?"

The woman agreed and invited Gina inside. As Gina drank a glass of water, the woman peppered her with questions. "What are you doing?" she asked. "And what are your goals in life?"

As Gina finished her water, she offered to pray with the woman. The woman requested prayer for her daughter, who needed a job and a cheaper car.

After her prayer, the woman had a change of heart and gave a donation for *Peace Above the Storm*. Gina went on her way.

A few weeks later, Gina was greatly surprised to receive a phone call from the same woman. She had called the phone number listed on the receipt and asked for Gina's contact information.

"Thank you for praying for me," she told Gina on the phone. "I'm calling because I wanted you to know that God answered your prayer. My daughter found a job and a good car too. And my daughter and I have been reading that book you left us, every day. It has been such a blessing to us!"

Gina's experience highlights the truth in the following statement: "The truth is to be sown beside all waters; for we know not which shall prosper, this or that" (*Christian Service*, 153). Even the most unlikely prospects are worthy of our time, attention, and prayers!

Later, Gina wrote that God had not only answered her prayer on the woman's behalf, but one of her own as well. That summer, she had been praying for God to show her how He was working through her. "And I saw it firsthand!"

The impossible happens

As Kristina Reeve entered a martial arts training center, a young man, probably in his twenties, came out of his office to greet her. He agreed to look at her books, and with each additional book she showed him, he became more and more excited. He was especially interested in her spiritual books, including *The Great Controversy*, *Peace Above the Storm*, and *The Ministry of Healing*, along with a few others.

"This is just what I needed!" he exclaimed. "God must have sent you here. Just last night, I was praying that God would show me the reason why I'm living and the right way to live, and today you show up with these books!" He went on to tell his story, sharing how he had been a foster child, taken in and treated like a son by the owner of the martial arts center where he now worked. "I need these books," he concluded. "How much are they?"

Kristina shared the price, and the young man went to get his wallet. A moment later, he returned, looking crestfallen. "I forgot my checkbook at home," he explained.

Kristina's heart sank a little. She had been so hopeful that he would keep the five books she'd shown him!

"But don't worry," he continued, "I'll figure something out."

For the next few minutes, Kristina waited patiently as the man tried everything he could think of to get his checkbook. He called his mother, who was busy and couldn't bring it. He called his brother, who had already left for work. He called his friend, who wasn't home. Finally, he had run out of ideas.

"Now what do I do, Lord?" Kristina prayed silently. "I'd love for this man to have these books!" Then she asked out loud, "Where do you live?"

"On Third Street," the man responded, to Kristina's surprise. She knew that someone on her team had another contact that needed follow-up who also lived on Third Street! She got directions from the young man and promised to meet him at his house at the close of her workday. He promised to be there, checkbook in hand.

Kristina left the shop hopeful but not confident. She knew that people rarely kept their word in situations like this: sometimes people weren't home as promised, their interest diminished, a significant other intervened, or a dozen other disappointing circumstances came up. All afternoon, Kristina prayed for the young man: "Lord, it seems impossible, but please help him to keep his word!"

That evening, when all the students had been picked up for the night, the team made their way to Third Street and located the young man's house. As Kristina knocked on the door, she murmured one final prayer. And, in direct answer to her oft-repeated prayer, the young man did keep his word! Not only was he home, but he also happily gave a donation for the five books he'd seen earlier that day.

As she rode home that evening, Kristina was thankful for two things. First, she was grateful that God answered her prayer. Second, she was grateful that while people are often fickle, God is always faithful! "God is not a man, that He should lie, nor a son of man, that He should repent. Has He said, and will He not do? Or has He spoken, and will He not make it good?" (Numbers 23:19)

Under the stars

The summer of 1995 is one that Steve Allred will never forget, because that summer changed his life in one very profound way.

Steve was 17 years old and "big booking," as the saying goes, with the Bible Story books in Salt Lake City, the Mormon mecca of the world. Just a few months before, Steve had acquired his first driver's license and was a certifiably dangerous driver in his 1981 manual-transmission Honda Accord. Since he still didn't know how to use the clutch without peeling out at most stoplights, his leaders found riding with him to be a bit terrifying, they later told him. More than that, it was his first summer as a colporteur. Even though Steve had never even heard a colporteur canvass in his life, much less given one, Bill Krick, the program head, had taken a chance and decided he would let Steve into the big book program.

In some ways, Steve was a shy and timid kid, so going door to door wasn't exactly his favorite thing to do. Going door to door for hours a day all by himself didn't make it any better. But he decided to do it anyway. He had his opening lines well memorized, and at each door he would ask people if he could set up appointments with them to return and make his sales presentation to sell his larger sets of books, which included The Bible Story set and a Conflict of the Ages set called the Bible Reference Library.

Week one of the ten-week summer program passed and Steve had not managed to set up any appointments. Thankfully, he did get out several of the smaller books each day, which provided him with enough funds for his gas and food. He chalked up his lack of appointments to the fact that he was new to colporteuring—and that none of the Mormons wanted his books anyway.

But when the second, third, and fourth week of the program passed and Steve had still not set up any appointments, he started to get worried. What was wrong? All of the other big bookers were getting appointments—and selling books—just fine. Why couldn't he even get any appointments? Steve's leaders were concerned as well, and asked Steve if everything was OK between him and the Lord.

One night, several weeks into the summer, all of the student literature evangelists were returning to the junior academy gymnasium where they were staying. It seemed that each of the other colporteurs had big smiles on their faces.

"I sold a Bible Reference Library today!" someone exclaimed, high-fiving another student who had also sold several sets. They were both excited and praising the Lord for the success, and rightly so.

Steve, on the other hand, slipped by everyone without being noticed. As he lay in his sleeping bag that night, out under the stars on the school patio, he poured out his heart to God. He talked to God about his fears and his embarrassment at not being able to sell any of the large sets of books. He asked God if everything was OK between them, and listened for Him to reply.

The sky didn't open up that night. But as Steve prayed night after night throughout those first five weeks of the summer, he learned to trust in God whom he had only known about before. All those nights under the stars during that summer in Salt Lake City changed his life in a profound way: he learned to pray. He learned about God who loves and comforts us when we're going through tough times. Today, Steve writes, "God brought me through that summer, and His faithfulness to me *then* is still a strong foundation for my trust in Him *now*."

What happened next really doesn't matter, but as it turns out, Steve ended up selling enough sets in the last four and a half weeks to make his scholarship check at the end a pretty good one. Sometimes God does give us what we want. What's most important, however, is learning the lesson that Steve learned: "God is our refuge and strength, a very present help in trouble" (Psalm 46:1).

Prayer opens doors

As Jessica Fields was leaving a house, she noticed that at the next house there was a woman talking either with someone in the backyard or on the phone, facing toward her. She was undecided. Gathering up her courage and praying for the Lord's support, she headed toward the woman. It turned out she was, in fact, talking to three people in the backyard, Jessica noticed as she got closer. Introducing herself as working on a scholarship project with a group of students, Jessica passed out the books to the group and began by canvassing the woman.

The woman interjected the canvass, however, and pointed to the elderly woman. She told Jessica that she would be the one to talk to. Jessica thanked her and began to focus on the older woman then, and all the while she had her back to a young man to whom she had handed a book when she first became acquainted with the group. She turned once, to briefly tell him about *The Great Controversy*, before returning to the nice, Christian elderly woman.

As Jessica spoke with her, the elderly woman explained to her that she didn't have any money and was also now faced with a broken-down car in her driveway. Feeling sorry for them, she reached for three *GLOW* tracts and a flier to some church meetings from her bag and handed them to the old woman. "These are for you," she said, handing them to her. "Thank you for your time." She then turned to leave.

"Go back and pray with them," the Holy Spirit spoke to her mind, as her back

faced the people she had just visited with. The thought felt uncomfortable and awkward since she had, after all, already turned to leave. She wrestled in her mind regarding whether to turn around and broach the subject of prayer or not, but she finally gave up and listened to the Spirit's promptings in that brief moment. She whirled around and asked, "Before I go, would you like me to pray with you?"

They told her their names and welcomed the prayer. After getting some hugs, she turned to leave again, but from behind her she heard a man's voice call, "Miss?" Turning to face the one who had called her, she noticed the man who had held *The Great Controversy* moments before, coming from around the corner of the house. Jessica was shocked, as he began to confess to her some of the struggles he had in his life and then to request, "Would you say a prayer for me?"

On the verge of tears, she choked out a prayer especially for him. As she was praying, she felt impressed that he needed *Man of Peace*, but he'd already said he didn't have any money to cover the cost of a book. After saying "Amen," she pulled out a pamphlet version of *Steps to Christ* and gave it to him, saying, "I want you to have this. I think it will help."

As Jessica continued down the road, she prayed that the Lord would provide extra donations to cover the cost of *Man of Peace* for the young man—a book she felt impressed that he needed.

Shortly afterward, she approached a home where the front door stood open. She knocked, and a man appeared. "Well, young lady, whatcha got?"

She showed him a few books, and he then gave her a donation—telling her to give the books that the money would cover to someone else. Leaving him with a pamphlet *Steps to Christ*, she thanked God in her heart and quickly made her way back to the other house. On the way there, she prayed that the young man, given a choice of books, would pick the book that he really needed.

He was still outside when she returned. "Hi," she said. "Someone gave me a donation and told me I could give a book to someone else," she told him. She then showed him *Man of Peace*. "This book has helped me to overcome my own personal struggles," she confessed to him.

"Then this is the one I need," he told her. As she was leaving, he said that he was going to start reading the book that day, and then would consider passing it on to someone else.

Praise the Lord!

Wherever you go

Aldavina Dos Santos didn't mind knocking on doors in low-income neighborhoods, or even middle-income neighborhoods. But for some reason, knocking on doors in high-income communities scared her. She dreaded walking through the gardener-maintained, perfectly manicured lawns and knocking on the towering doors. One evening, as she was working in just such a community, she met an elderly man who invited her inside. They talked for a while, and he gave her a donation for *The Great Controversy*. Suddenly, the man's wife appeared and snatched the receipt out of his hand. She looked flustered, as if she just couldn't believe her husband had just given money for that book. She waved Aldavina away, uninterested in anything she had to say.

"Ma'am, before I go, may I pray with you?" Aldavina asked, as the wife was quickly ushering her outside.

The woman's countenance changed, and she paused. "Well, yes. Yes, I guess you may," she responded. The three of them bowed their heads, each taking a turn to pray. Aldavina recalls that the couple both prayed truly beautiful prayers.

After prayer, the couple invited Aldavina to come by again if she was ever in the area. The husband also signed up for correspondence Bible studies. Generally, when an individual is interested in a correspondence study, a member of the local church will take a Bible lesson study guide by their house and drop it off. Then, they return a week later to pick up the first lesson and leave a second lesson. Each week, they make an effort to connect with the contact and build a friendship.

In most cases, the story ends as the student literature evangelist leaves the door, but in this case Aldavina had the opportunity to see the results of her labor firsthand. While she was working in that area, Aldavina was living with a family who were members of the local Adventist church. The couple she lived with volunteered to adopt the correspondence Bible study interest, the man she had met, agreeing to drop off a Bible study guide weekly.

When her hosts followed up with the elderly gentleman she'd met, they realized they had a mutual acquaintance. Aldavina's host family was renting a house that belonged to a friend of the man who wanted the Bible studies. The coincidence provided an instant connection, and the correspondence Bible study became a personal Bible study. Now, instead of simply dropping off a lesson each week, Aldavina's hosts would spend a hour or so visiting and studying the Bible with the man! In fact, they hit it off so well that they agreed to rotate the location of the Bible study each week—at Aldavina's hosts' house one week and the elderly man's house the following week.

Even though Aldavina dreaded working in the higher-income neighborhoods, she realized that God had needed her in that specific neighborhood for a reason. Her connection to her host family, and her host family's connection to her contact, made her God's perfect tool for that particular situation. God said to Joshua, "Have I not commanded you? Be strong and of good courage; do not be afraid, nor be dismayed, for the Lord your God is with you wherever you go" (Joshua 1:9). And now, Aldavina agrees. She writes, "If God is by my side, what do I have to be afraid of when I'm striving to win souls for Him?"

Fixin' for a change

Jennifer Calhoun approached a home where an older man with a blond beard sat on a broken lawn chair outside his garage. She showed him *The Great Controversy* and began to try to make friends with him.

"Do you have any religious background?" Jennifer asked.

"Well, I've been goin' to a Baptist church in town . . . but, lately, I've been fixin' for a change."

"What kind of change are you looking for?" Jennifer asked, curious.

"Well, Sunday is just the wrong day to worship. Saturday is the right day," the man explained.

"Really!" Jennifer exclaimed, astonished. "How did you come to that conclusion?"

"Years ago, while I was living in the world, I studied the Bible with a Seventh-day Adventist—and the Bible is just as clear as day: Saturday is the Sabbath. It's been in the back of my mind ever since, but over the last six months, I just kept thinking about it more. See, I've been listening to this Adventist radio station . . ."

The man, Jim, went on to explain that he had recently started keeping the Sabbath on Saturday at home and attending the Baptist church on Sunday. But just that morning, he had prayed about his conviction to keep the Sabbath, and that evening, Jennifer, a Seventh-day Adventist literature evangelist, showed up in his driveway!

Jennifer and Jim shared a wonderful visit. By the time she left, Jim was the new owner of *The Great Controversy*, *Peace above the Storm*, *Man of Peace*, and

He Taught Love. In addition, he signed up for personal Bible studies with the local Adventist church. As Jim discovered, "Never a prayer is offered, however faltering, . . . never a sincere desire after God is cherished, however feeble, but the Spirit of God goes forth to meet it" (*Christ's Object Lessons,* 206). When we decide we want to change to follow God, we will not be disappointed!

As clear as day

When Lorenzo Rolle started his first summer as a student literature evangelist, his main goal was to make enough money to buy a car. Yet, somehow, he also had the distinct feeling that God had some specific purpose for bringing him to the program in Calgary, Canada. For a reason unknown to him, he'd recently been thinking about studying theology. He mentioned the thought to his good friend and role model, Daryl St. Clair. "You should pray about it, Lorenzo," Daryl advised.

With all these thoughts tangled up in his mind, Lorenzo knelt to pray. "God, what do you want me to do?" he asked. "Why am I here?" Then he simply knelt there quietly, hoping God would respond.

The next afternoon found Lorenzo knocking on doors in Calgary. It was a rough day, so to keep his spirits up, Lorenzo moved as quickly as he could between the doors. On those sorts of days, he would ring the doorbell once and listen for footsteps. After a few seconds, if he heard nothing, he was off, running to the next door. At one particular door, however, he felt the impression to ring the doorbell a second time. He did, but hearing nothing, he took off across the grass.

As he was running across the lawn, he saw the door open and a man emerge.

"Oh, I'm sorry, sir!" Lorenzo called, returning to the door. "I thought you must be sleeping or not at home." He then launched into his presentation. After listening for a few moments, the man interrupted.

"What do you believe?" he asked. Once Lorenzo answered, he asked another question—and another. "Who do you believe God is? Do you believe in angels?"

Lorenzo answered each rapid-fire question honestly. Eventually, the man stopped. "I'm a pastor, you know," he explained.

"You know, sir, just last night, I was praying about becoming a pastor," Lorenzo confessed.

"Do it!" the pastor encouraged. "We need more young men today who can

.explain why they believe what they believe. Come on inside, won't you?"

Lorenzo stepped inside and canvassed the man on all his books. As he concluded his presentation, the pastor went in search of his checkbook. As Lorenzo watched, he told himself strictly, "Lorenzo, if this man takes all of your books, do not cry."

Eventually, the pastor found his checkbook. But instead of writing just one check, he wrote two. The first was made out to the student program, in an amount that covered the five books Lorenzo had in hand. The second check was made out to "Lorenzo Rolle," in the amount of two hundred and fifty dollars.

As Lorenzo gazed at the second check, he began to cry, in spite of his instructions to himself moments earlier. For, there, written in the memo line of the check, was God's direct answer to his prayer the night before: "Study Theology."

Lorenzo recalls, "That was a day I shall never forget. I'd never heard God speak so clearly in directing my path—it was as clear as day—and in writing!" Lorenzo now has a personal experience with God's promise in Proverbs 3:5, 6. "Trust in the LORD with all your heart, and lean not on your own understanding; in all your ways acknowledge Him, and He shall direct your paths."

5
Power of Persistence

"And let us not grow weary while doing good, for in due season we shall reap if we do not lose heart" (Galatians 6:9).

When the prophet Elisha was on his deathbed, "Joash the king of Israel came down to him, and wept over his face" (2 Kings 13:14). Though an idolatrous youth with little respect for God, Joash recognized in the aged prophet one whose presence provided stability and leadership to the nation.

The dying prophet, directed by the Spirit of God, desired to give to the young king one final lesson of faith. He instructed Joash to shoot an arrow out of the open window toward the armies of Syria, saying "The arrow of the Lord's deliverance and the arrow of deliverance from Syria; for you must strike the Syrians at Aphek till you have destroyed them" (v. 17). Then he commanded the king to take the bundle of arrows and strike the ground with them. Joash struck three times and stopped, to which the prophet responded, "You should have struck five or six times; then you would have struck Syria till you had destroyed it! But now you will strike Syria only three times" (v. 19).

Commenting on this story, Ellen White writes, "The lesson is for all in positions of trust. When God opens the way for the accomplishment of a certain work and gives assurance of success, the chosen instrumentality must do *all in his power* to bring about the promised result. In proportion to the *enthusiasm* and *perseverance* with which the work is carried forward will be the success given. God can work miracles for His people only as they act their part with untiring energy. He calls for men of devotion to His work, men of moral courage, with ardent love for souls, and with a zeal that never flags. Such workers will find no task too arduous, no prospect too hopeless; they will labor on, undaunted, until apparent defeat is turned into glorious victory" (*Prophets and Kings,* 263, emphasis supplied).

God needs people in these last days who will "not grow weary while doing good" (Galatians 6:9); who will persist in their efforts to reach the lost; who will work with a determination that will not fail or allow discouragement. Are you up to the challenge? "Here is the perseverance of the saints who keep the commandments of God and their faith in Jesus" (Revelation 14:12, NASB).

A second chance

Late one night, Jonathan Zita was tired and hungry, but his partner and he decided to knock on one more door. They were happy they did because they met a young woman named Linda, and her life has never been the same.

She did not look like someone who would be interested in anything spiritual. However, Jonathan and his friend still went through their usual introduction, and she actually let them in.

Once inside, Jonathan shared with her more of what they were doing in her community and also showed her one of their health books. She like it very much, so he proceeded to show her a spiritual book, *God's Answers to Your Questions.* Her face turned angry, and she quickly told him that she did not believe in God and didn't want his "God" book. She muttered something about her dad being killed and couldn't understand why God would allow that—if He existed. One thing Jonathan had realized over the years is that people often say quietly what really matters to them. All must learn to listen carefully and also learn that it's not always what is said that matters, but sometimes what is muttered or left unsaid.

Since she was young, Jonathan took a risk and boldly asked her, "If God exists, wouldn't you want to ask Him why He let your father die? As you can see from the title of the book, it might really answer your question!"

She refused the book, and they kept talking. After some time, she decided to take the book that dealt with health. Upon her return with the money, Jonathan's partner asked her if she really would not prefer the *God's Answers* book. It was evident that there was a struggle going on, but she then firmly declined.

After a long talk, it was time to go. Jonathan felt impressed to pray with Linda. He could sense that she was empty and needed the comfort and blessing of God. He told Linda, "I know you don't believe in God, but do you mind if I pray for you?" She smirked and told him that he could do whatever he wanted. He prayed for her health, her needs, and her future. It was a simple prayer, but he meant every word of it.

When he finished the prayer, she had tears in her eyes. She was quiet, and so they took up their bags and started to leave. She looked up and said, "Jonathan, I think I'm going to take the God book. I'm ready to give God a second chance."

There are many Lindas out there who need the opportunity to give God a second chance. They are empty, but they don't know where to turn. Linda had filled her days with smoking, drinking, and immoral activities. Yet, she knew there was something missing—a void that only God could fill. God wants to use you today to reach out to someone. Won't you make yourself available to Him?

You're here!

Raeann Leal knocked on a door, just as she had done hundreds of times before. She was surprised by a very welcoming smile and the words, "You're here." The woman, who said her name was Josie, continued, "You're the students, right?"

At that moment her husband arrived home in his car, and Josie waved her hands wildly and said, "The students are here, the students are here!" As he got out of his car, he exclaimed, "We've been waiting for you for so long!" Raeann was somewhat in disbelief. "We've been waiting for you students with the books for over a year now," said Josie. "What other books do you have that we don't have?"

Then the story was revealed. Four years earlier, a student had knocked on Josie's door, and she rejected him. The next year, she rejected another student. The third year, she got a *Final Events* DVD by Doug Batchelor; she watched it and loved it.

The next year, a student, Anna, knocked on her door, and Josie chose *The Great Controversy* for her husband. In January of that year, her husband finally picked up *The Great Controversy* and read it through twice; he was now reading it for a third time.

Raeann's leader arrived at this point and began talking to the husband. The husband was very excited. "I have never seen anyone more excited," the leader said later. "He was waving his hands."

The man then asked, "Why don't you guys come every six months instead of only once a year? How much money do you want for these books? I will pay you good money for them. Is twenty dollars for each one good enough?" He showed Raeann his extensive library of Christian books and then proceeded to choose six of her books and give a $100 donation. Raeann told the couple about the location of the local Seventh-day Adventist church and invited them to visit.

The very next Sabbath—only three days later—Josie came to church and sat with Raeann and her leader. After church, the rest of the students (about fifteen of them) met her, and she said to them: "You all should never stop doing what you are doing. I rejected the student two years in a row!" She added, "I recently talked to my pastor about the Sabbath, and my pastor told me to leave! The Bible has come alive to me this year more than any year in the last twenty years." With students gathered around, the pastor prayed for her, and when he had finished, she was crying. "This is what heaven is going to be like," Josie said, "with all these kind of people around you."

From unwilling to enthusiastic

A man opened the door and let Kristina Reeve get as far as the first book, *Health Power*, and then he yelled across the house, "Are you interested in any health books?"

"No!" his wife called back.

"I'm sorry," he informed her, "but we aren't interested right now. What religion are you, anyway?"

"I'm a Seventh-day Adventist Christian," she replied. He still wasn't interested in any books, so she dropped down to the pamphlet version of *Steps to Christ*.

"We can leave this book for a small donation." Kristina told him. "It tells how to have Jesus as a personal friend and Savior."

"No, that's OK. We deal with that," he answered, handing the book back. In a way that was quite unlike Kristina, she pushed it toward him again.

"Even just a few quarters or one dollar?" she pleaded.

"OK, come on in," he said with a sigh, opening the door. He left her standing in the doorway while he went to the kitchen. His little boy brought her a glass of water.

Kristina overheard a conversation.

"Have you seen my motorcycle keys?" the man asked his wife.

"What do you want them for?" she responded. He didn't answer but must have found them, because he went out the back door, around the house and down the driveway to a motorcycle parked on the street. Kristina wondered what he was up too. He pulled something out of the seat and then walked through the back door again.

"Here's a donation for you," he said with a smile, handing her ten dollars.

"For that amount you may choose a book!" she exclaimed, showing him five books. Praise the Lord, he decided on *The Great Controversy*.

Kristina rejoiced the whole way down the street. Nearing the end, she paused. *Do I hear something?* she asked herself. Yes—someone was calling her name! Looking back up the street, she saw the same man, sitting on top of his motorcycle. She ran back up the hill.

"I'm going to write you a check," he announced. "Whom do I make it out to?"

To her surprise and amazement, he wrote it for $40, trading that for the ten-dollar bill! He said that his wife wanted the cookbook. How he knew there was a cookbook, Kristina didn't know. He also chose *The Ministry of Healing*. They had a wonderful conversation. As she was leaving, he said, "I'm a Christian and am really interested in mission work. That's why I wanted to help you out. Keep up the good work, and I'll be praying for you!"

Persistence paid in full

Jaime Martin entered a small private business. On the walls were framed Bible verses and Christian quotes, so she felt as though this was a divine appointment. Feeling sure these people were Christian, Jaime showed the woman that she was with the company that produces the blue Bible Story books and asked if she had a spiritual background. To her surprise, she replied that she did not; however, she said that the owner was a Christian, and she directed Jaime to his office.

The owner was talking on the phone, so Jaime told him she could wait for him. After he got off the phone, she canvassed him, and he seemed interested in the books. Then he asked where she went to school. When he realized that she was an out-of-state student, he immediately began to shut her down.

"What did I say wrong?" she asked, trying to turn the situation around.

"You're an out-of-state student. I only support in-state students," he replied.

Changing the subject, she said, "I noticed you had Bible verses on the walls of your business. Are you a Christian?" He replied that he was, and then they began to have a discussion on religion and Adventism. He asked many questions, asking for a Bible reference with the answer. Silently praying, Jaime answered him as best as she could, showing him Bible references.

"You know your Bible," he said, surprised. "Not many people know their Bible these days."

He asked questions regarding the Sabbath, and why everyone else kept Sunday. Jaime showed him the book, *God's Answers to Your Questions*, but he was not interested in books. She kept praying that God would work a miracle and allow this man to get a book, but no matter what she said, he still refused to get a book and support an out-of-state student.

Impressed to leave him with the book anyway, Jaime laid it on his desk and told him that she would give him the book because it answered a lot of the questions he was asking, and that God would provide the money later. All of a sudden, he pulled out a large donation and handed it to her. Shocked, she stared at him as she realized God had worked a miracle on this man's heart right before her eyes.

"You were persistent," he said.

Jaime gave him a copy of *The Great Controversy* as well, knowing that he needed those books. "I'll read them," he promised.

Leaving the business with joy, she could hardly believe that she had actually experienced what had just happened. Just as God is persistent in trying to reach our hearts, He wants us to be persistent in reaching other people's hearts for Him.

An open heart

While Cassie Dhole was canvassing in Las Vegas, Nevada, she met an older woman named Janet. When the woman opened the door, she quickly stepped outside to shut out the noise coming from inside her home. Cassie for some reason didn't open with a neutral book like the cookbook but began to canvass her on *Steps to Christ*. The woman was very interested and said it would help her. So she went back inside to grab her checkbook.

When the woman returned, Cassie introduced her to *Man of Peace*. "I love that one, too, but unfortunately I can only help with ten dollars," she explained.

"These books go together because they are a devotional set," declared Cassie, hoping that she would be willing to spend just ten dollars more.

She then proceeded to disclose why she couldn't spend more. Eventually taking off the beanie she wore, she explained how she had been struggling to fight breast cancer for years, which left her both penniless and hairless. After sharing her story, she asked what church Cassie belonged to. Cassie shared with her that she was a Seventh-day Adventist. And right then her face lit up and she exclaimed, "No way! I've always had Jehovah's Witnesses or Mormons come by, but never a Seventh-day Adventist. I watch 3ABN on my local channels, and I love your religion!"

Right then, Cassie knew she had to share more material with her. So she pulled out the children's books, since the woman had grandchildren, and she loved all of them. The now thrilled woman then asked if Cassie had cookbooks, since she knew Seventh-day Adventists have a health message. Cassie showed her the cookbook, and she loved it! Then, she went on to show her prophecy material and gave her *Final Events of Bible Prophecy* by Pastor Doug Batchelor first. She looked at it and said, "He's my favorite preacher! I watch him as much as I can." And last, Cassie brought out DVDs and *The Great Controversy*. Right then, the woman decided that she needed all of the books now, no matter how it might affect her finances.

She helped out with a generous donation to cover the books and to help with Cassie's education. She also signed up for personal Bible studies and agreed to pray before they separated. This experience teaches that one never knows who is waiting to meet them with open arms and a ready heart!

Words of kindness

While working in a middle-class neighborhood, Keri Scau met a middle-aged woman unloading her groceries. Keri's assessment was that this person had the means to afford the books; she only had to stir up interest. After presenting several options from children's stories to cookbooks and still receiving a hard no, she offered the smallest book, a pamphlet version of *Steps to Christ*. For that book, most usually ask for a small donation of two to five dollars.

"Whatever you feel like giving helps me go to school." Again, a hard no. Keri was ready to wish her well and go on her way. Instead she gently asked, "Well, before I go, is there anything I could pray with you about?"

The woman burst into tears and out poured a story of her terminally ill child. It ended with a prayer and a hug and her marveling, "How did you know to pray with me?" A divine appointment indeed!

People all around are hurting, and we can never know just how much a kind word, thoughtful act, or a prayer can comfort their hearts. Ellen White affirms this as she says, "Words of kindness, looks of sympathy, expressions of appreciation, would to many a struggling, lonely one be as a cup of cold water to a thirsty soul" (*Counsels for the Church*, 127).

"Do you really believe this stuff?"

Anca Chirvasuta noticed two women painting the front of their house as she walked toward them, books in hand. "Looking good," she said, greeting them with a big smile. "How are you today?" They turned to look and momentarily stopped working to inquire what this young woman was doing showing up uninvited on their front lawn and interrupting their project.

"Well, my name is Anca, and I'm a student working my way through school," she happily answered as she began to give them the canvass she had given countless other people throughout her canvassing career.

Only this time, Anca was interrupted by one of her new acquaintances with, "Hold on, do you really believe in this stuff?" The woman pointed to the books Anca was in the middle of presenting.

"What do you mean?" Anca asked, needing a second to get her bearings and process the question.

"I mean, do you really believe this–this whole 'God thing'—that He even exists?" she snapped back, giving a critical eye.

"Why, of course I do. I really do!"

"What makes you believe in God, anyway?" Anca could hear the harsh skepticism in her voice.

"Well, ma'am," she started, darting a quick prayer while trying to speak meekly and yet confidently. "I believe in God because of the way I have seen Him change my life. You see, without God in my life, I would've been a lost cause. He's the One that has given my life purpose, meaning, and incredible joy."

Anca must have continued to share like this for another minute or so, getting more and more excited from the reminder of what God *has* done in her life through-out the years, and that she had so *much* she could share, when it suddenly dawned on her that her listener's countenance had softened. Instead of the intimidating scowl she had given a minute ago, a smile had appeared, and Anca was confused and stopped talking.

After a pause, the woman smiled again and said, more softly this time, "I, too, am a Christian but am so sick and tired of pretend Christians that I wanted to see if you were really genuine. Here's something to help you out." And with that, she pulled out a fifty-dollar bill and handed it to Anca with, "You keep doing what you're doing."

This beautiful story illustrates the power of a simple yet sincere testimony of faith. Unlike this case, not everyone who asks us the reason for the hope that is within us will be "secret" believers, and even fewer may open up their wallets to donate to a cause, but each testimony that we bear carries some sort of impact, whether for the Kingdom or for ourselves. May our life testimonies not only be an influence for good through our words and profession but even more through our kind demeanor and Christ-like actions.

Connections

One day Gerard St. Hilaire canvassed a particular neighborhood in which everyone happened to be Jewish and rejected him at every house.

"What's happening here?" he began to question God.

Walking up the street, he saw a car with a parking permit from his state university. *I have to canvass this house and find out this student's information!* he thought to himself. He knocked on the door, but there wasn't anyone home.

"I'll come back later," he said to himself.

Finally completing that street, Gerard anxiously ran back, stopping the car as it pulled out of the driveway. To his delight, he discovered her name was Jillian and she did indeed go to his school and knew a few of the same people. After speaking briefly to Gerard, the student drove away, and he once again confidently proceeded to the front door. He rang the doorbell and stepped back.

"Hello!" Jillian's mom greeted as she opened the door.

"Hi, my name is Gerard," he began, introducing himself and explaining what he was doing.

"Not interested!" she responded.

Despite her disinterest, God knew that Jillian's mom needed those books and continued to work on her heart. As soon as she spoke those two words, Gerard enthusiastically replied, "I know your daughter. We go to the same school!" Jillian's mom then invited him into the house, and she chose to get two books plus *Peace Above the Storm*.

The once doubtful canvasser then realized that no one else could have reached that woman. He was sent there because of what he had in common with her daughter. The Bible says in Psalm 32:8, "I will instruct you and teach you in the way you should go; I will guide you with My eye."

Comforting a mother's heart

The radios were going off with other people calling in books left and right, but for Jeandra Martin it was a dry, discouraging day. She was glad for the others who were getting books out but wondered and asked God if He was going to use her that day.

Pressing on, she reached another door and knocked, but nobody answered. She went to the side door, an unusual decision for Jeandra, since she tended to skip side doors if she had already knocked on the front door and nobody seemed to be home. This time a woman on the phone came to the door; her eyes were bloodshot and glassed over from crying.

"Now is not a good time," she said and started to swing the door shut. Jeandra knew this woman needed some peace, so she quickly stuck the book *Peace Above the Storm* through the door into her hands and said, "I know you're busy, but I would just like to leave this with you as a gift." She accepted it, and Jeandra knew God would provide extra money to cover the gift later.

Thinking nothing more of it, Jeandra moved on, and as she stood on the porch of the next house, the woman she had just shared the book with opened her side door again, called out and waved her over. *Is she going to give the book back?* Jeandra wondered as she hurried down the steps and back to the previous house.

"Please, come in," the woman invited and began to apologize for her shortness earlier.

As they talked in her house, she poured out the sad story of how her daughter had run away with her abusive boyfriend, and she had no idea where they were. She had just been on the phone with her husband trying to decide what they should do next to find their daughter.

Their whole family history was one of dysfunction and pain, and she described how just the previous night she was sitting outside looking at the stars, wondering where God was in her life and in the crisis going on. Now able to comfort the distraught mother, Jeandra shared how God has promised to be there always and never give us more than we can handle.

They prayed together, and as she wiped her tears the woman asked about the book Jeandra had given her and what she was doing. Jeandra told her about her scholarship and mission, and the woman pulled out a donation for her so that Jeandra was able to leave her with another book called *He Taught Love*.

As Jeandra left, the woman thanked her profusely and said, "This is just what I needed. God sent you here."

Warmed by this thought, Jeandra was reminded that God always has a reason for everything, and even though she may have to go through discouraging times, He has specific people for her to minister to. Even if that was the only person she encouraged that day, it would have been worth it.

Discovering God's plan

Lindsay Longo sat sobbing in the closet. The feelings she had endeavored to keep hidden now poured forth in a torrent of tears. What on earth was she doing in the middle of winter, seven hours from home, knocking on doors eight hours a day, sharing Christian books?

A few weeks earlier, her friend Jonathan had asked her to join some of his academy and college students for a canvassing blitz, a one and a half—week stint of colporteuring in Roseburg, Oregon. Lindsay was 15 years old and had done some canvassing but didn't enjoy it. However, she was flattered that he would ask her to come. So despite her dislike of the work, she had agreed to go.

They started canvassing on Sunday. It was raining quite a bit, which made keeping their books dry quite a challenge. Rejections were many, and by the end of the day Lindsay was miserable thinking of having to survive eight whole days of that. The next day wasn't much better, and Wednesday morning found her completely despondent and depressed about the prospect of facing another door and saying another canvass.

All Lindsay wanted to do was go home, but she had given her word to be there the whole time, so quitting wasn't an option. Besides, there was no one to take her back early even if she wanted to leave. She was stuck. So, as was her habit in every trial, she called home.

Lindsay's poor mom tried to console her as she sobbed out her feelings, her dread of the day, and her hate for the rejections. Her mom shared many Bible promises, of which Lindsay couldn't remember one. Then Mrs. Longo prayed for her, and Lindsay finally retorted, "Fine, but that doesn't change the fact that I still have to go out and knock on doors all day."

At the end of their conversation, Lindsay's mom told her she had been chatting with Katie who was in Africa at the time. She said, "Katie is praying for you for a certain number of books and a certain amount of money today," but didn't say what the goal was. After thanking her mom, Lindsay promptly dismissed the thought from her mind and proceeded to go about the day in utter misery.

The first street where Jonathan dropped her off was the longest street she had seen in her life. At the first door, a dog barked and barked and no one answered. She thought, *Good, one less person to reject me.* At the next door, however, a woman answered the door. As soon as she found out Lindsay was a Christian student, she started to tremble, and a little tear welled in her eye as she gave Lindsay a big hug and invited her inside.

She was a woman that Lindsay could tell was sensitive to the Holy Spirit. She shared that she had been reading the *Left Behind* series, but she couldn't get through it because she felt like something was wrong with it.

Noticing her need, Lindsay showed her a few devotionals, adding, "And the book *Left Behind or Sincerely Taken* by Louis Torres talks about the rapture."

Completely emptying her bag, Lindsay showed her the children's books. Although the woman didn't have kids, she wanted the books for her nieces and nephews. Finally, looking through the books again, she decided to get all the devotionals, *The Great Controversy*, *Left Behind or Sincerely Taken*, and two copies of all the kids' books, adding up to sixteen books.

Lindsay closed her on all the books, giving her a donation range of $160 to $240. She wrote a check for $250 and handed it to Lindsay. Remembering the other books in the van, she pleasantly responded, "Well for this you can get our other books too!" So she added *Patriarchs and Prophets*, *Final Events*, and all the other books they had.

At this point the woman had twenty-three books, which her donation had more than covered. But she said, "I want to give you more money."

"No," Lindsay said, "I'm not out here for the money!"

"I know," she replied, "but I still want to give you more money."

"But I'm not out here for the money, you've already given more than enough!"

She then said with authority in her voice, "I feel like God is calling me to give you more money."

What can a person say to this? "Well, if God is calling you," she said, "but I just want you to know I'm not out here for the money!"

She nodded and took back the check she had written for $250 and wrote out a new check for $300.

Lindsay sat there dumbfounded. The most books she had ever gotten out in a day was perhaps fifteen, and here she had just gotten twenty-three books!

Before Lindsay left, the woman signed up for Bible studies and told her, "I just want you to know that I know God sent you to my door today. I'm not usually here and am so busy, I never have time, but today I did, and I know God sent you here."

She then prayed for the young canvasser, asking that wherever she went she would hear a voice saying, "This is the way, walk ye in it."

Lindsay was deeply moved. Her depression and discouragement were gone. She realized at that moment that God had a work for her to be doing in canvassing. God had called her to this work for a special reason.

A mysterious miracle

It was almost lunchtime when Jennita Schmidt came to a gas station. She walked into the convenience store and began canvassing the first cashier. When she told the cashier they were leaving the books on donation basis, the cashier handed the books back, explaining that the owner did not allow soliciting in the store, and that she could not get them on the job. She pointed to the room behind her, saying, "My boss is in there, and if she sees me doing this she will be mad."

Normally, boldness is one of the things Jennita struggles with in canvassing, and if she senses resistance or if someone asks her to leave, she usually quickly pulls out the smallest book offered to people who aren't interested, or she leaves. But this experience was different. Even though the cashier's words were suggesting Jennita should leave, Jennita knew that deep down the worker did not want her to leave and that she was really interested in the books.

Jennita continues the story. "I could not bring myself to leave that one hungering person. I continued showing her different books, and several times while we were talking she quickly set the books down when she thought her boss was coming or when she had to help a customer, but she continued to listen as I told her more about the books. I just knew that God wanted me there."

As Jennita continued to talk with the cashier, a coworker walked by, and the woman called him over to look at the books. He quickly pulled out a twenty-dollar bill and picked *The Great Controversy* and *Peace Above the Storm*. After he left, Jennita turned back to the young cashier. "Which of the books interested you most?" she asked.

"I want all of the books, but I only have five dollars, and I really can't get anything here," she replied.

Perhaps seeing the co-worker get two books impressed her even more that she needed to get at least one of them. Jennita knew she would make a decision soon; the struggle was written all over her face. *Dear Lord, please help her to make that right decision,* Jennita earnestly prayed.

"Come to the back of the store," were her next words.

When they met there, she handed over five dollars and picked out *God's Answers to Your Questions*. The "no-soliciting" ice was broken, and she thanked the canvasser for coming.

"God has a purpose for everything," the cashier stated with a mysterious look on her face.

She stood silent for a minute, then pulled out another five dollars, handed it to Jennita with a hug, and then left.

Jennita left that gas station awed at what she had just seen. God had worked right before her eyes, taken control of the situation, and worked a miracle. Suddenly it hit her how small her efforts are in comparison to God's power, and it was humbling to see the simple means that God uses to accomplish His purpose.

I'll meet you in heaven!

A young woman that Kristina Reeves spoke with decided to get one of the Spanish books. Before she got her money, however, she called her dad to come and look at the books. He knew more English than she did, so Kristina and he started talking.

Slowly looking at each English book, he began asking all kinds of questions about different topics. He didn't seem interested in getting anything, so Kristina wanted to leave. Surely there was someone else on this street waiting to get books.

Kristina began praying that he wouldn't ask about her religion, because that would start a new topic and detain her even longer. However, God had other plans. The man asked what religion she was, and that turned into a mini Bible study on the law and the fourth commandment, Jesus' sacrifice, and salvation. He had heard about Seventh-day Adventists, disagreed with their beliefs, and didn't want anything to do with them. After a long discussion, Cestmir drove by in the van and waved.

The man stopped their discussion mid-sentence. "Was that your leader?"

"Yes." Kristina answered.

"Oh no! I'd better let you go! He's going to be upset at me for keeping you so long!"

Before Kristina even had a second to think, she heard herself speaking words totally unlike her!

"He won't be upset at you if you get three books from me."

"Three books!" he gasped. "I wasn't planning on getting any!" He sighed loudly. "Let me see which ones you have again. How much are they anyway?"

She smiled. "If you get three, I can give you a discount."

"I like this *Health Power*. How much is it?"

Kristina quickly stacked *God's Answers to Your Questions* and *The Great Controversy* on top of the *Health Power*. "How about these three? In fact, I'll make you a deal. I'll give you one for $15, two for $25, or three for $30."

He chuckled. "How about two for $20?"

"No," she answered in as serious a voice she could muster, "I said two for $25 or three for $30."

He put the *God's Answers to Your Questions* and *Great Controversy* back on the table, so she placed *The Ministry of Healing* and *Peace Above the Storm* on top of the *Health Power* in his hand and repeated, "One for $15, two for $25, or three for $30."

Kristina was really praying now and very surprised at herself for acting this way. She re-canvassed him on the books, sharing how much they had blessed her life and how she was confident that they would draw him closer to Jesus as his personal friend.

Finally he threw his hands in the air. "OK, I give in. I'll get *Health Power*, *Ministry of Healing*, and *Peace Above the Storm*. Let me get my checkbook." He laughed quietly and said, "You know, you are a really good salesman, and I like you. You really know the Lord, and I wish all teenagers were as good as you."

They prayed together, and then he asked for the address of the Adventist church where the canvassers were staying. "Maybe I'll go visit it sometime," he said with a grin.

Just then, Cestmir drove up with the big van—it was time for pick-up. But the man stopped her one more time. "I'm going to meet you in heaven," he said, smiling. "And when I see you, I'm going to come running up to you and say, 'Kristina! Kristina! Do you remember me? I'm the man who got three books from you!' "

Searching for peace

One day while canvassing, Elias Ortega was praying for a divine appointment. At one house the woman barely cracked the door. He introduced himself and asked for her name. She looked pretty mad and said she didn't want to give her name.

Elias started canvassing her through the crack in the door, but after he presented the first book, which was *Peace Above the Storm*, she said, "I don't want anything. I'm just about to go buy groceries."

The door was slightly open now, and Elias could sense she was still upset. Nevertheless, he showed her the economy version of *The Great Controversy*.

"I can't even get that," she said. "I have the exact amount of money needed for groceries."

Continuing to show her even the smallest book, *Steps to Christ*, she angrily refused. She began to ask questions, like who he was, where he was coming from, and which company he was working for. Elias showed her his school ID and explained the program to her.

Elias explains this part of the story: "I told her it was for school and a scholarship. I explained that even the smallest donation would be appreciated. She still refused, but after we talked a little more she agreed to help and accepted the *Steps to Christ*."

She went inside to get the donation, and when she came back she asked if she could see *Peace Above the Storm* again. Describing it to her again, Elias could sense that she liked it, but she gave it right back. After talking a little more, she decided to take it and went inside again to get the money. Elias was feeling ecstatic because she had refused a total of six times!

When the woman returned, she was crying. She told him she had been scammed before and that she never opens the door to strangers, but for some reason she opened it for him. He seemed nice and genuine, so she had not slammed the door on him.

Then she related about her past experiences. Her nephew was a nice guy but then started using drugs and had gotten a girl pregnant. He dropped out of high school and didn't have a job. His life was spiraling down. He had tried to stay with the her, but she told him he needed to be with his parents.

She explained that she was divorced and living alone. Often feeling lonely, every day had become a struggle, and she couldn't find peace in anything. When she heard about *Peace Above the Storm*, though, she said something told her the peace she wanted was there.

Elias prayed with her, and she squeezed him tight, thanking him, because she didn't think she would ever find peace. She believed there was a reason Elias came to her door. Truly this was a divine appointment!

Last door experience

When I (Kamil) started canvassing that day, there was no way I could've imagined what lay in store for me. I canvassed for several hours, but strangely, no books went out! Not one. My lunchtime arrived, and I wondered at such a unique beginning. Quite unusual. Though I'd never had this experience before, I encouraged myself with the thought that there were still many hours in the day in which to get books out. Surely things would change.

After lunch, I resumed canvassing, but strange things now began happening. I met people who were interested in the books, but somehow at each door they were never able to get the books! I began to notice a pattern. After they shared they were interested, they would leave to go get their donation but could never find any money. They would discover that the wife had the checkbook, or their wallets were missing, or the wallet was left with someone. In one way or another, they lacked any money to offer as a donation. This scenario played out over and over again, and it seemed to me that something supernatural was going on and preventing people from getting books. The day was extremely exceptional and trying as I prayed that God would use me to get books out that day.

By evening, I began running. I wanted to be ready for any home that lay ahead with people who would be ready with a donation for the books that would change their lives. After seven o'clock in the evening, there was still no sign of success. I began running faster. Eight o'clock came and went. Still no books.

Finally, just before nine o'clock, my leader came by to pick me up—it was near ending time. I looked in the vehicle and realized that I was going to be the first student picked up that evening. I quickly suggested to the leader that he pick me up last. The leader agreed and began picking up all the others.

Meanwhile, as I was running from house to house in a lower middle-class community, I noticed a longer driveway lined with trees leading to a very nice home. I whispered to myself, "Thank you, Jesus. I just know that these people will want to get Your books!"

But after a quick rejection, I was running down the driveway and on to the next house—running a little faster because time was running out. I was not willing to end the day without getting at least one book out!

A few doors down the street, I met a nice woman who, while listening to me, noticed several mosquitoes flying around her porch light. She quickly interrupted my canvass and invited me inside.

There I made friends with her husband and shared with them about my journey from the Czech Republic to the United States to attend a Christian school, and then on to the books I was sharing in the community. They were so impressed with what I shared that they ended up getting sixteen books for their home and wrote a check for $200! Finally! Someone was able to find a donation!

I walked out of the house beaming, and with my heart praising God that I was able to leave those precious books in that home! I had waited for a blessing *all day long*, and when it came, it was overwhelming! God had saved a day's worth of blessings for the last door.

6
God's Timing

" 'Are not five sparrows sold for two copper coins? And not one of them is forgotten before God. But the very hairs of your head are all numbered. Do not fear therefore; you are of more value than many sparrows' " (Luke 12:6, 7).

Cornelius was a Roman centurion of the Italian Regiment who worshiped the God of heaven to the best of his ability. The Bible tells us he "prayed to God always" (Acts 10:2). God knew the heart of Cornelius, and when the time was right, He sent an angel to guide him to the apostle Peter. Cornelius was then directed to send servants to Joppa, where the apostle was lodging in the home of a tanner named Simon. Through a series of events, Peter was led to return with the servants to Caesarea, where he preached the gospel to the household of Cornelius and baptized them.

Jesus *knew* the particular address where both Cornelius and Peter were living. He knew the experience each one needed in order to grow. When He saw that the timing was right, He arranged matters so that each would receive the maximum blessing He could give them. The fact is that He is intimately acquainted with the needs of every human being. He even has every hair on our heads numbered.

God still works on His timetable, and His timing is perfect. When laboring with Christ, we will often be brought in contact with a particular individual or family whom He has prepared to receive the message of truth. We are encouraged that "Jesus knows us individually, and is touched with the feeling of our infirmities. He knows us all by name. He knows the very house in which we live, the name of each occupant. *He has at times given directions to His servants to go to a certain street in a certain city, to such a house, to find one of His sheep*" (*The Desire of Ages*, 479).

And in His perfect timing, He planned for you to read this next chapter at this time!

A mama's prayer answered

Laura Rupsaite looked up and down the dingy street where she had been dropped off. She wasn't even supposed to be there, but when her canvassing leader's car started having serious trouble before they could reach her assigned territory, she decided to find a place to canvass near the mechanic's shop.

It was a lonesome street of old trailer houses high on top of a hill, and not exactly the most desirable community with families and kids for a guaranteed successful canvassing day. But she and her leader said a prayer, and off the canvasser went. Loathing in her mind the prospects of the day, a clear Bible text cut across her trail of thinking: "What good can come out of Nazareth?"

When Laura knocked at the first door on the right hand side, a lovely woman opened the door. It turned out that she was an Adventist Christian who had been trying to reach out to her family and neighbors, seemingly in vain. She got a few books as witnessing tools, and before Laura went on her way, they had a heartfelt prayer. The woman prayed for her neighbors to receive the message books, as well as a special request for her son, who had walked away from God years ago and got into many destructive addictions.

Laura felt encouraged by that encounter, and as she proceeded down the street, many of the neighbors indeed opened their hearts and got books with the message of Jesus. It was such a blessing!

A couple of hours later, as the darkness was starting to fall, Laura was walking past an old house a little off the road in a field. It was clearly long abandoned as the grass around it had grown up tall, the paint of the house was chipped and worn, and the windows were boarded shut. In fact, it gave off an uncomfortable ghost-town feeling, so she started walking faster.

All of a sudden, a noise seemed to come from the direction of the house. Laura quickened her pace, trying to get down toward the next house. But a thought that somebody might be in the old house started to taunt her. "Skip a house, skip a blessing!" The stuff she'd heard in training was coming back to her. *What if somebody is in there? What if they really need what I have? What if this is God telling me to go and just check?* Questions pestered her mind. Reluctantly, but not able to resist the impression, she turned around and started to walk back toward the house.

As she came closer, she realized that indeed someone *was* inside! Carefully climbing up the broken staircase, Laura breathed a deep breath of prayer. She knocked on the door and quickly pulled back a few steps. The sounds inside the house stopped, and after a few moments the door swung open with a cloud of smoke and all kinds of smells gushing out at her.

As it cleared up, she saw a massive frame with a hairy face standing in the door right in front of her, "What do you want?" She froze for a second, and then, remembering the unusual inclination to come to this house, she sent up another prayer and started pitching the man with her usual canvassing script.

For a while he just stood there with a startled facial expression as if she was completely out of context with whatever he was doing. Then he brushed off all that she had said with, "I don't cook, don't have kids, don't like to read, and I am not religious! What are you doing here?" Heidi's logic was telling her to just go away, but she couldn't, because by now she was sure there was some special purpose for this encounter, and she wasn't going to leave until it was discovered!

Racing through her thoughts for what to say next, her could only think of *The Great Controversy*. She was well aware that it was the largest reading book she had in her bag, when he wasn't even a reader! Even so, she said, "Sir, I have a book just for you!" and put the heavy volume right into his hand. She launched into telling him all about what the book meant to her and how it applied to his life. His face changed from distant carelessness to moved interest. The atmosphere grew solemn. Finally, he said, "I think I need this book."

Laura was stunned.

Taking *The Ministry of Healing* out of her bag and stacking it on top of *The Great Controversy* in his hand, she said, "I think you could use this book too! It talks about how to overcome addictions!" His laughter dispelled any remaining tension as he glanced back inside the house at a table laden with empty bottles and cigarette butts. "I think you might be right! How much for both of them?"

While pulling the money out of his wallet, the man said, "It's really strange that you got me here today! I live in a different town altogether, and I just came here for an hour to visit my old friend. I used to live here some thirty years ago. But if you go up this road, to the very top of the hill, the very last trailer on the right, my mom lives there. She is a really good Christian woman; she will get all the books off of you!"

As Laura was working through the remainder of the street that evening, she could hardly wrap her head around the incredible workings of God in an effort to save us. She could only imagine how, as this woman was still praying for her son a couple of hours before, God ordered an angel to fly swiftly to where he was and encourage him to go meet up with his friend in some abandoned house just along the way where she was going. All the detail, all the mercy and providence, some thirty years of praying—nothing is overlooked by God in seeking and finding that which is lost. It's sobering how God can plug us into His plans.

Her final request

On another occasion, Heidi Young was staying back at church because of kitchen responsibilities. Suddenly impressed that she needed to canvass, she grabbed her bag and began canvassing the neighborhood near the church. One place she went to was a small school. The front door was latched tightly, so she tried persistently to get someone's attention, but nobody came to let her in. Giving up on that school, she began to walk to the next place.

As she walked away, Heidi saw a woman sitting in a car in the parking lot. She was about to bypass her but was reminded that this might be the person she needed to talk to. Approaching the vehicle, Heidi noticed that the woman was talking on her cell phone, so she just stood there and waited. The poor startled woman jumped as she noticed a stranger standing next to her but rolled down her window. Heidi then handed her *Peace Above the Storm*. After she had told her about all the books, the woman decided to get the message books that Heidi had shown her.

After she received the books, she began to explain that she was just about to kill herself and told about the five knives that she had with her that would do the job. Continuing, she further related that the phone call she had just made was a message to a friend explaining what she was going to do and was saying goodbye. She had planned that this would be her last phone call.

The woman said that before she had made the phone call, she had prayed to the Lord and said, *"Lord, if You really care for me, You have to send someone to me now."* The woman got her answer! She promised Heidi that she would read the books. It was wonderful to be used by God in such a way.

The preacher

It was a cold day. People were rushed and snappy. Yet Jennita Schmidt plodded through her day canvassing in a Walmart parking lot.

Am I wasting my time? Thoughts of discouragement rumbled around in her mind.

For sure we have plenty of other business besides this wind-blown parking lot! she continued with a sigh.

"Lord, if you want me to stay, please reveal Your will to me," she pleaded. It didn't seem as though God had any purpose for her there, but maybe there was a least one more person she needed to talk to. In less than two minutes, a man walked up to her, handed her a ten-dollar bill, and walked away. That was enough! Soon she was approaching a pickup truck and waving to catch the attention of the person inside.

The window rolled down, and a friendly smile greeted the anxious canvasser. While conversing with the man inside, she noticed a Bible open on his lap. She commented about it briefly and then canvassed him on *Man of Peace*, *God's Answers to Your Questions*, and *The Great Controversy*.

Thoroughly curious, she decided to ask him what he was studying in his Bible. His answer almost caught her off guard: "I'm preparing my Christmas sermon for Sunday!" he said.

Re-canvassing him on *Man of Peace*, she read him a paragraph containing this quote: "There is nothing, save the selfish heart of man, that lives unto itself. No bird that cleaves the air, no animal that moves upon the ground, but ministers to some other life. . . . But turning from all lesser representations, we behold God in Jesus. Looking unto Jesus we see that it is the glory of our God to give" (*The Desire of Ages*, 20, 21).

Interrupting her as she read the last sentence, the man exclaimed, "Do you know what the title of my messages is? 'The Gift That Keeps on Giving.' " She was about as pleasantly surprised as he was! He continued: "I have no doubt that God led you here just while I was preparing my sermon, and I know He set up our meeting."

Jennita wholeheartedly agreed. And now, all three of those books are in his home!

Pleading eyes

Jaimie Douville felt as though she was walking through a desert. Long, dry stretches of slammed doors, empty homes, or uninterested occupants spurred her on her way down the endless length of asphalt. She yearned for just one soul to refresh her spirits with an interest in her Savior. She thirsted to see *them* thirst for the water of life! But yet, these walks in dry places are never without an oasis.

Jaimie found one precious oasis experience that gave her light feet for hours. Her name was Stacy—heavyset, college-aged, short red hair, and spiky piercings. She came out from a wild, overgrown backyard at the sound of the weary canvasser's knocking. As Jaimie started her canvass, she first showed her the cookbook. The two chatted a bit. And Stacy seemed enthusiastic about the book. However, when the conversation transitioned to a spiritual book, she wrinkled her nose.

"That wouldn't interest me," she said decidedly.

"Oh, OK," Jaimie replied casually. "Do you not have much of a religious back-ground?" She hoped to find out more.

"No," Stacy answered lightheartedly. "But let me get my mom to look at this cookbook." Stacy disappeared behind the peeling blue house and came back a few moments later with her cheerful mother.

"Hi, I'm Barb," she said. Stacy had already told her mother about the cookbook, and Jaimie showed her the other health book too.

"Stacy, go grab my checkbook," Barb asked. "We'll get these." Once Stacy had disappeared, Jaimie felt impressed to broach the religion topic with Barb.

"So . . . " She paused until Stacy was out of earshot. "Does your family have a religious background?" The corner of Barb's mouth curled down a little.

"*I'm* religious," she said. "I go to church regularly, but my three girls . . . well, I didn't raise them in church, and I kick myself *every day* for that because none of them feel a need for church or God. They don't see it as being important. But I really wish . . ."

Just as Jaimie handed her *The Great Controversy*, Stacy returned with the checkbook. Barb's mouth closed sadly, as though she had unsuccessfully approached the topic of religion with her daughter before and been defeated. She handed the stack of books—two health books and *The Great Controversy*—to Stacy and began to fill out a check.

"How much are you going to give her?" Stacy asked, peering over her mother's shoulder.

"Twenty-five," she responded. "We'll get the two health books."

"Oh. Well, I want to help too," she mused. "And what's this book?" She suddenly noticed *The Great Controversy* on top of the stack.

"That's my favorite book," replied Jaimie, a silent glance passing between her and the mother. "It covers the last two thousand years of history, showing how Bible prophecies have been fulfilled." Stacy listened as Jaimie set aside her rehearsed script. "I read it about a year or two ago, and it really woke me up to see the times we're living in. When you look at Bible prophecy, it shows just how relevant the Bible is for our times today."

"Yeah, the Bible is important," added Barb, who looked as if she was about to pop from earnestness. Her eyes bored into the other's, silently pleading. *Please, talk to her! She won't listen to me, but she'll listen to you.* So Jaimie did. Stacy listened, and for a few moments Jaimie shared her testimony.

"OK, I'll get this book," Stacy said after a minute. She pulled ten dollars from her purse. "But if it's not good, I'm gonna call you up." She chuckled a bit as Jaimie wrote a receipt. "It's a good thing you came just now," she continued. "We are just leaving to go get a new puppy."

As they said their goodbyes, Barb didn't say much, but her eyes were bursting with gratitude. The look of a mother's fond hope, seeing her irreligious daughter with *The Great Controversy* clutched beneath her arm, became etched in Jaimie's memory. At that moment, the dry stretches of desert were forgotten, and the slammed doors seemed so insignificant.

"I will open rivers in desolate heights, and fountains in the midst of the valleys; I will make the wilderness a pool of water, and the dry land springs of water" (Isaiah 41:18).

The disadvantaged, determined missionary

Jensen Ruud cleared his throat. It was time to start another day of canvassing, but his voice was becoming progressively softer. *How am I going to canvass if I can't talk?* he thought to himself. He knew that if he didn't take a day to rest, he could risk having a weak voice for several days instead of just one. However, God might bless his efforts and heal his voice if he just stepped out in faith and began to canvass. With this thought, Jensen asked for God's blessing and decided to try.

Relying on God's strength and the little bit of voice he still had, he started his day. The first street was a struggle. It was hard to speak, and nothing happened for the first hour. But as he approached his next assigned area, he notice an abandoned building with a car parked out front. The front door was unlocked, so he stepped inside.

"Is anyone here?" Jenson called out.

A female voice responded from a back room. He shuffled around piles of paper and pieces of furniture scattered around the room as he went to meet her.

Soon he found a woman, introduced himself, and showed her one of the recipe books. The woman suddenly became very solemn.

"My husband passed away a month ago," she said bluntly.

Thinking back to one of the roughest times in his own life, Jensen quickly handed her the book *Peace Above the Storm* and began to relate his experience, telling her how that book had been a comfort to him after the death of his father. He suddenly saw how God was using him—a willing yet disadvantaged missionary. The two walked over to her cluttered desk, and Jensen listened as she poured out her heart.

Her husband had contracted a mysterious condition that put him in the ICU for two months. Eventually he passed away, leaving this woman with more than a million dollars in medical bills. She had stayed with him the entire time, leaving only once in the two months to get something from her house.

There they sat, the two of them in the nearly empty building where she had run her real estate business. She had let it go by the wayside during the ordeal and recently picked it up again. God had blessed her mightily. When she was considering selling her home to pay the medical bills, her neighbor had offered to buy her house before she told anyone of her intentions. Her real estate business became more successful in a month's time than it had been before the ordeal. The bills were quickly being paid off.

"I learned how to pray without ceasing," she explained. God truly had carried her through that experience.

She eventually got all six message books, including *Peace Above the Storm*, *The Great Controversy*, and *Ministry of Healing*. Before parting ways, they prayed together, bringing the hurting widow's burdens to God and thanking Him for His goodness.

God only asks that we give Him what we have. Jensen may not have been able to speak very well, but the woman didn't need someone to speak to her. She needed someone to listen and to care as Jesus does for us.

A tearful encounter

Jennita Schmidt stepped into the first business of the day, a tiny yellow tobacco shop. A woman stood behind the counter talking on the phone. The tone of voice, expression, and teary eyes revealed that things were not going well. Yet she desperately tried to hide it as she greeted Jennita.

"How are things going?" asked Jennita gently.

"Not well at all," she replied, wiping away another stubborn tear.

Sensing she did not really want to share, Jennita began introducing the books. She opened with *Man of Peace*, emphasizing the personal life of Jesus—how He dealt with temptation, sorrow, loneliness, and rejection, giving us a perfect example of faith and trust in God. The woman clasped the book, and, without waiting to hear the rest of the canvass, she nearly thrust the money into the surprised canvasser's hands, crying, "I need this book!"

Just then a customer walked in, so Jennita thanked her and prepared to leave. But just as she was ready to step out the door, she felt very convicted. *How can I just walk away from this hurting person? How would I feel if I was hurting and someone just walked away without giving me a solution to my problem? What if there is no one who'll tell her they care?"*

She immediately returned and waited until the woman finished serving the customer. Again Jennita walked up to her. "I know you are going through something tough; is there anything you would like me to pray for?"

"Just pray for me, please!" she begged.

"May I pray with you right now?" Jennita asked.

The woman responded by coming over to the other side of the counter. Jennita placed an arm around her and began praying as the tears were now pouring down the burdened lady's cheeks.

With the prayer finished, the now teary-eyed tobacco-shop employee gave her the biggest hug, thanking Jennita and expressing how much the prayer meant to her. What a joy it was meeting such a precious young woman that day.

Sent from heaven

A car drives up to the house that Lori-Anne Wilson is about to canvass. The driver steps out, knocks on the door, and begins speaking with the owner of the home. Not long into their conversation, the owner steps back into his house, and both Lori-Anne and the visitor wait. Using these few moments, Lori-Anne begins to canvass her, starting with *Peace Above the Storm*.

The woman glances up. "You are heaven sent; this is exactly what I need." She explains further that her sister had passed away two weeks prior to that, and she is just having a hard time dealing with it.

Besides purchasing a book, and although already a Christian, the woman also requests Bible studies.

Delighted to find someone looking for Jesus and the peace that only He can give, Lori-Anne finishes by praying with her. The encounter shows Lori-Anne just how important the canvassing work is. There are so many broken people who need someone to reach out to them.

Prophetic encounter

Westney White felt discouraged. He and his leader had met many interested people, but none of them seemed to have money for the books. Just before he chose to give up on that section of houses, the Lord impressed him to keep on going just a little farther.

Westney relates the story: "I came to a house, and the man that opened the door looked like a gangster. He was tatted up and had a rough exterior. Surprisingly, he invited us in, and we talked to the family and showed them all the books.

"At the end of the presentation the wife asked me to repeat the price for the set they were interested in. I told them the price again, and she gave a few excuses and asked if they could do payments.

"The husband interrupted. 'How much?' I told him the price again, and he went upstairs and brought back the full amount in cash!

"As I was filling out the paperwork, the husband began to tell me that he didn't really believe in God, but that he wanted his four young children to have a better life than he had growing up.

" 'I wouldn't have gotten the books if it hadn't been for my co-worker,' he explained. 'Every day he gives me a ride to work, and every day he tells me about Jesus and his love." His face got serious. 'Yesterday on our way to work, my co-worker told me that the next day someone would come by my house with books about the Bible. And you came to my door just like he said.' I was shocked. He continued, 'I still don't know about this whole God thing, but I think He is making me a believer.'"

God knows just the place His missionaries need to be at the right time. What a wonderful choice Westney made to keep going. By doing that, he found a man whom God was already working on.

On restricted territory

One morning, Jensen Ruud's leader dropped him off near a small set of industrial businesses. The directions were short: "There's not much here, but go ahead and do them anyway."

He hopped out and advanced up the dusty road to the first building. Outside were several people working. The first one he spoke to was delivering soft drinks and snacks. He was not interested, but he directed Jensen to a man on a forklift painting the side of the building and warned him not to go inside of the factory.

"They don't allow anyone from outside in there," he said.

Jensen continued on to the man painting and began canvassing him. "I'm broke! I'm painting this factory for nearly minimum wage," came the reply. "I'm usually unemployed, and I just recently got this job, but you could speak to Michael. He's inside of the factory. He may be interested."

Earlier that morning, the canvassing leader had trained them on using names to enter places. "All you need is a name!" he enthusiastically told them. "If anyone asks you what you are doing, just give them the name. Don't say anything else! God has a divine appointment for you!"

The recently employed man had just given Jensen a name to use, but he too warned him not to go inside. Approaching the side door of the factory, he peeked inside. Both of the men, who didn't even work inside of the factory, had warned him not to enter. But God had given Jensen a name to use. He seemed to be opening doors.

If I used the name, what would I do once I got inside? I don't even know the person! Questions pestered his mind. Eventually, he decided that God's guidance was a good enough reason to enter.

Acting confident, Jensen entered the factory. The entryway was empty. He continued walking in to a large open area where the work was done. Nearby, around a square table, were five people in a seemingly important meeting. He shrank from the thought of interrupting them, but the name came back to mind. Doing his best to appear confident, he walked up to them and asked to see Michael. They eyed him suspiciously, but then one spoke up. "Michael? He's over here. Let me take you to him."

The man walked him over to a worker and introduced him, then walked off. Michael was a middle-aged, heavyset man with red hair. His shirt had several Bible verses listed on it. It wasn't surprising that he took an immediate interest to the books.

The two had a powerful spiritual discussion in the midst of flying sparks and heavy machinery, and Michael eventually picked out *The Ministry of Healing* for his family. More than that, he directed Jensen to other people to talk to in the factory and the nearby buildings.

Of all the people Jensen could have been led to, God led him to the one man who had an interest in His truth. He opened the doors to enter places that Jensen never could have reached. Definitely that book will be useful to save someone for eternity.

Why are you back?

Cody Smith scanned the neighborhood where he and his friend had just been sent. *I recognize this place, and, yes, that house over there,* he said to himself. Memories from two years earlier raced through his mind.

All that time ago, on a particular day, Cody had walked up to that very house. He remembered a party was going on, attended by a father and mostly teenage boys. When he showed them the books, they laughed and made fun of both him and the books.

Now, as he worked along the street, his mind kept going back to that house, and everything in him wanted to skip the house. But as a soldier for Christ he knew his duty; he must canvass that house. He knocked on the door and looked around. Everything was the same. The cars, the yard, the house color, and the furniture on the porch were the same.

Before he could think of walking away, the same father who had been there two years before answered the door. Scared, Cody began his canvass but was soon interrupted. The look on the man's face was intense curiosity, and he stopped Cody and asked, "Didn't I meet you before?"

Cody answered half-heartedly, "Yes, about two years ago."

The curiosity hardened into something like the cement beneath his feet. "So why are you back? Is something so important?"

Sucking in his breath, he answered, "Yes, sir, your salvation is important, and if I could come every day, I would."

As he finished, he realized he was looking this man in the eye with no fear. The man's stony face softened, and he said, "Wait there and sit down."

After a few minutes, the man brought every young person from two years earlier outside to sit and listen to everything the persistent visitor had to say. By then, everything in Cody's mind was telling him that they would make fun of him as before. But as he showed them each of the books, they made no sound, instead showing great interest in the books. Something inside his mind said to push *God's Answers to Your Questions*.

As Cody gave the canvass for *God's Answers to Your Questions*, they stopped him and began asking questions on death, heaven, the Sabbath, and other topics; and for each answer, he showed it to them in the book. The father was completely shocked, and quickly gave the full donation for the book.

"May I pray with you before I leave?" Cody asked.

The entire group stood up and held hands reverently as Cody proceeded to pray for them.

Sharing with an attorney

Kristina Reeve walked through the halls of a large business building. She had just parted with the last two copies of *The Great Controversy* in her bag; however, she decided to finish that building before calling for more books.

On the third floor, an attorney looked at the health book, then set it down and motioned her into his office. "I'm tired of working and need a break, so I'll talk to you. Have you heard about the Supreme Court ruling yesterday on the banning of the Pledge of Allegiance in public school?"

He pulled out the newspaper and began to show her what it said. Kristina wanted to get going and not waste time, but God impressed her to keep talking and making friends, steering back the conversation to the books every chance she got. He asked her questions like "What are you doing?" "What kind of school are you raising money for?" and "What religion do you believe?"

Their conversation then steered to the Bible, which led him to tell her that he was Catholic. Then he suddenly asked Kristina if she had read the previous week's *TIME* magazine. He said there was a whole article on Daniel and Revelation, but it made no sense to him.

"I need to study Daniel and Revelation and see if I can understand them," he concluded. Immediately Kristina thought of *The Great Controversy*, but she didn't have any in her bag! She quickly called for more books, but her leader was out of radio range. So she canvassed the attorney on the book anyway, and he wanted it. Kristina also showed him *God's Answers to Your Questions*, and he liked that one as well.

"What is the difference between Seventh-day Adventists and other Christians?" he questioned. "And what do you believe about Holy Mother Mary and the apparitions?"

The two had a complete Bible study as Kristina earnestly prayed for wisdom. Then her leader called on the radio and brought *The Great Controversy* to the building. She ran downstairs to meet him.

When she came back up to the attorney's office, she discovered that he had already started reading *God's Answers to Your Questions*—the chapter on the Sabbath, of all things! She was shocked! He finally decided to get both *The Great Controversy* and *God's Answers*. Kristina knew that God had just worked a miracle.

7

Angels Among Us

"But to which of the angels has He ever said: 'Sit at My right hand, till I make Your enemies Your footstool'? Are they not all ministering spirits sent forth to minister for those who will inherit salvation?" (Hebrews 1:13, 14).

During the time of prophet Elisha, when the king of Syria was seeking the destruction of Israel, the Lord, on multiple occasions, revealed the king's battle plans to the prophet, enabling the Israelites to evade the enemy armies. After several failed attempts, the king began to think he had a traitor in his ranks. When he attempted to ferret out the traitor, he was told that it wasn't his soldiers who were giving away his battle plans, but "Elisha, the prophet who is in Israel, tells the king of Israel the words that you speak in your bedroom" (2 Kings 6:12).

When the king heard this, he sent his armies to the city of Dothan, where the prophet was staying, to capture him and bring him back. Early the next morning, when Elisha's servant arose and went out of his house, he saw the city surrounded by Syrian soldiers, horses, and chariots and panicked. " 'Alas, my master! What shall we do?' " he asked.

The calm reply from the man of God came. " 'Do not fear, for those who are with us are more than those who are with them.' And Elisha prayed, and said, 'LORD, I pray, open his eyes that he may see.' Then the LORD opened the eyes of the young man, and he saw. And behold, the mountain was full of horses and chariots of fire all around Elisha" (vv. 15–17). Unseen by human eyes, perceived only by the prophet's eye of faith, God had provided an army of angels that excel in strength to protect His faithful servants.

The Bible tells us that we are regularly surrounded by the presence of these holy beings. Every human being has a guardian angel at their side. Jesus, speaking of those new in the faith, said, "In heaven *their angels* always see the face of My Father" (Matthew 18:10, emphasis added). And the psalmist encouraged, "He shall give His angels charge over you, to keep you in all your ways" (Psalm 91:11).

There have been occasions when, like the servant of Elisha, people's eyes have been opened, and they have been enabled to behold these majestic sentinels. Sometimes, as in the case of Elisha, they appear as beings of fire and light. At other times, they may appear in human form, as the angels that visited Abraham before the destruction of Sodom. This is why we are admonished not to "forget to entertain strangers, for by so doing some have unwittingly entertained angels" (Hebrews 13:2).

"We need to understand better than we do the mission of the angel visitants. It would be well to consider that in all our work we have the co-operation and care of heavenly beings. Invisible armies of light and power attend the meek and lowly ones who believe and claim the promises of God. Cherubim and seraphim and angels that excel in strength—ten thousand times ten thousand and thousands of thousands—stand at His right hand, 'all ministering spirits, sent forth to minister for them who shall be heirs of salvation.' Hebrews 1:14" (*Christ's Object Lessons*, 176).

Praise God He has not left us to do this work alone! What do we have to fear? May we take courage as we walk the narrow path with our angel by our side!

Canvassing with an angel

Kayla Marcoux was canvassing a strip of six businesses. The businesses were divided by a small grassy area, with three on one side and three on the other.

Kayla began to visit the first set of businesses. She was rejected by the first two, but the third did give her a small donation for a pamphlet version of *Steps to Christ*. As she came out of that third business, she noticed a man sitting under a tree in the grassy area. She canvassed him, and he gave a donation for two items—*The Great Controversy* and the *8 Laws of Health* DVD. She then passed the grassy divide and went on to the fourth business.

As she was attempting to canvass someone at the fourth business, the man who had been sitting under the tree entered the business, bringing someone with him.

He told the man, "You need to give her ten dollars."

The man did so, and Kayla gave him a copy of *The Great Controversy*.

The man from under the tree then began speaking fluent Spanish to the people at the business where Kayla had been trying to canvass. He was bilingual! He could speak to them in their native tongue.

The man then apparently told the people in the fourth business to give Kayla ten dollars also, and each of them did! And she gave them books.

As they left the fourth business, the man asked Kayla, "Have you been to all of these businesses?"

"Just the first three," she replied.

"Did they get anything from you?" he asked.

"Not really," replied Kayla.

"Let's go back to them, then." The man then proceeded to take Kayla back to the first businesses at which she had been rejected. After that, they went to the other two that she had not yet visited.

In every business she went to, every person that she met gave a donation of $10, and Kayla gave him or her a book. After visiting the six businesses, she had given out twelve books.

Kayla wondered who the man was, because the people did not seem to know him. They asked, "Is this your father?" To which she would reply, "No. Just a friend."

At the end of the last business they canvassed, the man said, "God bless you," gave her a hug, and turned to leave. In a bit of a daze, Kayla began walking down the street. She glanced back to offer a quick "thank you," but the man was gone. She did not see him again.

Looking down at her bag, she noticed that she still had one *Great Controversy* remaining in her bag. She never carried more than two copies at a time, but she had given out at least five! How could that be?

When she realized what had happened, she called her leader and sat in the van weeping for some time.

The day before she had showed up at the program—about a week before this incident occurred—Kayla had fasted and prayed for an entire day, asking God to give her love for the people and to bless her ministry as a student literature evangelist. I would say He did. He had walked with her!

Expected

During one of Cassie Dhole's canvassing days, she came across a Mexican restaurant. She approached the man at the counter and quickly ran through her canvass, since he seemed disinterested from the beginning and the restaurant was exceptionally busy. After only a minute of sharing, he told her that he wouldn't be getting anything. She thanked him for his time, and, turning to go, she heard a man call out to her to wait. She turned back and saw a man cooking in the kitchen, looking her way. He wanted her to wait for him to come out.

So she waited. As five minutes ticked by, she began to get anxious and wondered if he was only wasting her time. Perhaps she should continue on. However, God impressed her that this situation would be worth the wait, no matter how long it would be.

After what seemed like ten minutes, the man walked out and suggested they sit at a booth so that she could show him the books. She began sharing in broken Spanish about *He Taught Love*, and he seemed to really like it. Then she shared the Spanish *Peace Above the Storm* with him, and he really liked that one as well. She began to close him on those two books, but he leaned over the table and began to point to the English *The Great Controversy* in her bag. He asked, "What is that?" Although she only had a copy in English, he still wanted to see it, so she handed it to him and called her leader to bring her a copy in Spanish.

As they waited for the leader to come, he scanned the first chapter intently.

Before long, her leader, who was fluent in Spanish, walked into the restaurant and handed him the Spanish *Great Controversy*, which is an abbreviated version of the English book. The man noticed that the Spanish version was not the entire book, and he was not interested in getting only half of the book. He handed it back to her leader.

Her leader then explained that they also had the book *God's Answers to Your Questions* in Spanish and ran out to grab it for him. He was very interested in that one and decided to get that one in addition to the other two that he liked.

When he came back with his $30 donation, he looked somewhat serious. Her leader turned to him and, in Spanish, thanked him for helping. The man then began to tell him a story in Spanish.

As the story progressed, her leader stared in amazement and said "Ooh" and "Ah" several times. Cassie wondered what was being shared. After the man had signed up for Bible studies and had prayer with them, they at last turned to go, with a peace resting in their hearts.

Once outside, her leader turned to her and shared that this man had felt for about a month that he needed to come back to Christ. He was raised Catholic but never really had a relationship with God for himself. He had said that two weeks before she came into the restaurant, a woman he had never met before had come in and told him that a girl would be coming by in two weeks with *exactly* what he needed to read to get to know God. He said that as soon as he saw Cassie, he knew this was the one she was talking about.

Cassie believes that angels not only work beside us at the doors, giving us protection and guidance, but they also go ahead of us to ripen the hearts of those we will meet with our precious books.

"I've seen these books in a dream!"

It was a day like any other, full of the sweat and weariness of going door to door in hot sultry summer weather. It was on such a day that Valerie Crosier experienced one of the best experiences of her life. She became part of a miracle.

As she sauntered up to the very ordinary looking house to knock, she did her usual quick prayer: "Lord, please be with my mouth. Teach me what to say at this door, fill me with love for this person, whoever they may be. They are Your child too."

She knocked, but it seemed that no one was coming. Would this be an exercise in futility? Then the door opened and she was face to face with a woman in her mid-fifties. She looked tired and worn out, with the "Why are you here?" expression Valerie had seen so many times before.

"Hello! My name is Valerie, and I have something special to share with you! Let me take a minute to show you what it is!" She opened the book *God's Answers* to *Your Questions*. The simple outline of questions on Bible topics followed by Scripture references for the answers was easy to canvass. And there was one part, in particular, that she loved to show everyone.

"Look here," Valerie said, smiling and pointing to the pictures of the fearful-looking creatures of Revelation and Daniel. She started to launch into saying, "Bible prophecy is scary to most people, but this makes it simple!" But while she was still in mid-sentence, the woman grabbed the book from her excitedly. "You aren't going to believe this!" she exclaimed. "I have seen this before! These very pictures were shown to me in a dream I had. I had no idea what they were at the time, but now they are here before me in this book! These exact pictures! I have to have this!"

Valerie stood amazed. Had God just used her to fulfill a plan for this woman that was marked out for her before she even arrived at her door? Was she a puzzle piece in His plan for this woman? For her to know in advance that what Valerie had to say was just for her, He actually showed her ahead of time in a dream these very pictures? It was truly amazing and humbling to her, for she had been going along as usual, unconscious of the awakening Spirit of God that was working on the hearts of the people she was yet to meet. Never did she forget that moment, the joy and wonder that lighted up the stranger's face, and the thought that God would do something so personal for her.

They both took a moment to praise the Lord for the amazing thing He had done that day.

He will open the blind eyes and free those who are in spiritual darkness. And He may use you to do it when you are least expecting it.

Cancer-stricken woman

One day, Marc went down an alley that had very few houses on it. The majority of the houses were fenced off, but he was able to talk with someone standing outside of their home. When Marc was finished talking with them, he was a little unsure as to where to go next.

At that moment Marc heard a voice that said, "Come out," so he began to walk out of the alley. On his way out, he saw a girl who looked like one of the students in his literature evangelist program. She was wearing a white dress with a blue belt and had a canvassing bag over her shoulder and a walkie-talkie in her hand. With the walkie-talkie she motioned toward one of the fenced-in yards. Marc took note and headed to the house she was pointing to.

He went up to the gate and began knocking and calling out. A woman came out and said, "I don't want anything!"

The young man said, "I'll be really quick!" The woman did not seem convinced but was curious to see who had come to her door. When she came closer to Marc, he noticed that the woman was bald. As they began to talk, he realized that she had cancer. She told him that she was dying.

Marc then began showing her the books *Peace Above the Storm*, *Man of Peace*, and *He Taught Love* and explained that the books were on how to find peace. The woman was amazed and asked, "How did you know to come to my door? No one ever comes to my house, not even my priest who knows I'm dying. And how did you know that peace is exactly what I need right now?" He told her that the Lord had ordained that he meet her that day. The woman got the books and expressed how grateful she was that Marc had come to her gate.

As Marc was walking away from the house, he called the team leader on the walkie-talkie and thanked her for sending the other student to point him in the right direction. However, the leader responded, "Marc, that student is not on our team today!"

Marc insisted, "No, I know that I saw her." He went on to give the description of what she was wearing and explained that she had pointed him to the house where the woman with cancer lived. The leader responded by saying, "She really is not on our team today. She is in Aiea, about thirty minutes way."

Marc saw someone that day, but we won't really know who or what it was until we get to heaven. We do, however, know that God is not "slack concerning His promise, as some count slackness, but is longsuffering toward us, not willing that any should perish but that all should come to repentance" (2 Peter 3:9). God sees those in desperate need of Him, and He will do whatever it takes to reveals His love and character to them.

"And one for your big friend"

One summer day, Cauvin Moreau jumped out on a street he would do by himself. One family he met requested two of his books. After handing him a donation, they offered him water. He gratefully accepted, and they returned with two water bottles.

"Here's one for you, and here's one for your big friend," they explained, peering around Cauvin, looking for the other guy who had now gone.

Cauvin had already had a similar experience several weeks before; so this time he asked what his friend looked like. They replied, "Well, he was light-skinned with dark hair, and wearing a light shirt and khaki pants. He was really tall, and could hardly fit in the doorway! He had his arm around your shoulder while you were talking, but he just left."

Stunned, Cauvin thanked them and went to the next door. There, a man got a devotional about the life of Jesus and then handed Cauvin two more water bottles—a small one and a large one.

With a smile on his face, he said, "Here's one for you, and this one [the large bottle] is for your big friend."

In awe, Cauvin left the home and called his leader, Jonathan, and explained what had happened. Jonathan in turn called his boss, Bill, and Bill suggested they return to the second house and ask the man for a description of this "big friend." When they did, the house was completely dark. After knocking several times, they peered in the window and realized that the house was unoccupied—completely vacant.

Jonathan began to question Cauvin about the man who got the devotional. He described him as a tall, light-skinned, dark-haired man wearing khakis and a white shirt. Suddenly both young men realized that this was the identical description the neighbors gave of Cauvin's "big friend."

Now a quick side note. When that group of canvassers finds people who make donations for the books, they give a receipt on which they write their name for the customer to know which student they helped. There is also a line for the customer's signature, but they only use it for credit card sales. So when Cauvin realized that the customer matched the description of the angel, he suddenly reached into his wallet and pulled out a receipt. With shaking hands he told Jonathan of how the tall man had taken the receipt pad from him and signed his name on it. The signature was unreadable, but they believe that they have the signature of an angel.

"I've seen you in a dream!"

Daniel Miranda was canvassing in a trailer park when he came across the home of a Pentecostal woman. She told him that she did not have any money and that she made money by selling food in the streets.

When he heard that, it really moved his heart with compassion toward her. He could see that she truely didn't have much.

He gave her an understanding nod and turned to leave for the next home, when she suddenly stared intensely at him and spoke. "I think I saw you in a dream last night! I saw many people, but the only face I can remember is yours!"

Daniel felt skeptical. Had she really had such a dream? Many people today claim to have dreams when all they want to do is to deceive you, he thought. Nevertheless, he knew God had sent him to her door and decided that he could, at least, agree with her that it was no coincidence that brought him there that day.

As he shared that God had indeed sent him to her door and showed her a Spanish *Great Controversy*, her face lit up. "I know what you have is good," she told him. She quickly bustled him into her home, seated him, and asked him to wait while she looked for a donation. She went from room to room, trying to gather together as much as she could. At last she put together the $10 she wanted to give—completing it with quarters. It was as though it was her last "measure of flour" that she had at home to share which enabled her to get this precious book. As Ellen White wrote, "The book *The Great Controversy*, I appreciate above silver or gold" (*Colporteur Ministry*, 128).

Daniel was just about to offer prayer before leaving when she chimed in, "Why don't you pray for us before you leave? I saw in my dream that before you left, you prayed with us and that at our house some would accept and some would not."

She called her children, and that was exactly what happened. The son was receptive to prayer, but the daughter was very reluctant. Daniel asked God to bless their home and left with peace in his heart for the divine appointment that God had orchestrated.

As Daniel looked back on that experience, he could tell it was of God, for the spirit of Satan would not lead someone to get *The Great Controversy* or be willing to be prayed for. He praises God for this divine appointment and encourages every canvasser not to forget that God is always near to us, whether the day is going great or not. All those rejections should be an encouragement. They show us that the divine appointment is getting closer, that God wants us to reach that house as soon as possible, and He does not want us to waste our time with those who are not receptive. Canvassing is more than sharing books and receiving donations—it is a ministry, soul to soul, heart to heart.

Let us always remember this promise: "Have I not commanded you? Be strong and of good courage; do not be afraid, nor be dismayed, for the LORD your God is with you wherever you go" (Joshua 1:9).

The ferocious dogs

Nicole Crosier was working her way down a street when she heard vicious barking farther down the street. Looking on ahead, she saw a high chain-link fence with two huge dogs throwing themselves against the fence and the high gate in an effort to get out. She continued working, praying her leader would come get her before she got down the street that far.

When she had finished canvassing the house before the one with the vicious dogs and was now walking toward that home, she prayed, "Lord, I can't even open the gate to this house without those huge dogs throwing themselves against it. If you want me to go there, You're going to have to send an angel to lead those dogs behind the house."

The moment she finished her prayer, the two dogs, who had barked ferociously and thrown themselves against the gate and fence incessantly the entire twenty minutes she had worked toward their house, turned and bolted from the fence as if in terror as she approached. They ran as fast as they could away from the gate! She watched as they disappeared behind the house. She rattled the gate cautiously, but they didn't come back. Slipping the latch open and quietly sneaking through, she tiptoed onto the porch and tapped on the door ever so lightly. Realizing no one would even hear her, she then worked up the courage to knock harder.

The woman who answered the door didn't even look at her. She walked out past her and looked around her yard. "How did you get past my dogs?" she asked incredulously. "They bite everybody!"

Nicole couldn't think of an answer except the obvious. "I knew you needed what I have, so I prayed, and God sent an angel who took the dogs behind the house."

She looked at Nicole as if she still couldn't believe she was standing there, took the *Steps to Christ* she offered, and promised her she was going to read it!

A dream about a bird and a flower

Kay Sanchez was canvassing a young Hindu woman whose husband was a new Christian. She had no interest in any of the books, however, so Kay dropped down to the *Steps to Christ*.

As she extended the book, the woman's hands started to shake as she held the book. "This is the book I need right now," she stammered.

"Yes, this book will really bless you," Kay agreed.

"No," the woman replied, "you don't understand. I had a dream about this book. I just had a dream about this book. This is exactly what I saw—the bird and the flower. I know I am supposed to get this book."

She got a donation for Kay and took the book!

God is truly doing an incredible job of paving the way for canvassers. We are only a tool in His hand!

Angel help

William MacArthur, a sincere young man who really loved Jesus, met a geologist who claimed to be a Christian but didn't believe in the biblical account of creation. William promptly pulled out his little notebook of Bible studies and began to share with the man how it doesn't make sense to believe only part of the Bible and reject other sections.

After hearing him out, the man, who had appeared uninterested the whole time, pulled out his wallet to make a donation for an *Ancient Dream* DVD. Surprised, William asked the man why he wanted it!

He explained, "Your Bible study was pretty boring, and I hate it when people preach at me, but the big shiny guy came from across the street and made me pay attention. He told me to listen to you, and then he went to the next house."

At the next house, William placed two books. Angels prepare the way for us and convict hearts that are hard and would be closed to our human logic.

"In working for perishing souls, you have the companionship of angels. Thousands upon thousands, and ten thousand times ten thousand angels are waiting to co-operate with members of our churches in communicating light that God has generously given, that a people may be prepared for the coming of Christ" (*Testimonies for the Church*, 9:129).

I had a dream . . .

At one door, Linda Chavez showed the man a cookbook and started to explain its benefits.

The man stopped her mid-sentence and said, "You're doing this as a ministry, aren't you?"

She replied with an affirming "Yes!" He went on to ask her if her team drove certain vehicles and then started to describe the people on her canvassing team as if he had seen them before.

Linda, awestruck, asked how he knew who was on her team. The man explained that he had just had a dream about Linda and the team the night before.

Excited, Linda handed him a *Peace Above the Storm* and began to canvass when he interrupted her once more.

"That's not the one," he said. He spread out the books in Linda's hands and pulled out a DVD she carried on Daniel chapter 2, titled, *The Ancient Dream*. "This is the one I saw in my dream!" he exclaimed.

Immediately, he ran inside for money and received the DVD. God had been preparing the way for Linda to knock on this man's door. It is so amazing to think that the Lord truly does go before us as we knock on doors. He has been working on their hearts long before we get there. In fact, He's been working in their lives since they were born!

8

Other Ways to Reach Souls

"To the weak I became as weak, that I might win the weak. I have become all things to all men, that I might by all means save some" (1 Corinthians 9:22).

The capital of ancient Attica and of modern Greece was Athens, situated in the southeast extremity of the Roman province of Achaea. Athens was the home of such philosophers as Sophocles, Socrates, Plato, Aristotle, and Demosthenes. The focal point of the city was the Acropolis, a hill about five hundred feet high, and the site of several famous temples. On a lower hill, to the west of the Acropolis, rose the Areopagus, or Mars' Hill. It was from this location that the apostle Paul, seeking to find an avenue to approach this elite class of thinkers, chose to employ a pagan altar dedicated "TO THE UNKNOWN GOD" (Acts 17:23) to arrest their attention and turn them to the God they were not yet acquainted with—the Almighty Jehovah.

There's no silver bullet in evangelism—no "one way" that works in every given situation. The great apostle Paul was in the practice of varying his approach to reach the particular people he was seeking to minister to, in order to save as many as possible. Ellen White comments, "To the Gentiles, he [Paul] preached Christ as their only hope of salvation, but did not at first have anything definite to say upon the law. But *after* their hearts were warmed with the presentation of Christ. . . . Thus when, melted and subdued, they gave themselves to the Lord, he presented the law of God as the test of their obedience. This was the manner of his working—adapting his methods to win souls" (*Evangelism,* 230, 231).

In the same way, we should always evaluate our methods of reaching the lost. While we should avoid adopting methods that would misrepresent our faith, we need to work to develop methods that will increase our influence with the people we are trying to reach.

"Very much more might be done for Christ if all who have the light of truth would practice the truth. There are whole families who might be missionaries, engaging in personal labor, toiling for the Master with busy hands and active brains, *devising new methods for the success of His work. . . .* My brethren and sisters, take an active part in the work of soulsaving. . . . By personal labor reach those around you. Become acquainted with them. Preaching will not do the work that needs to be done. Angels of God attend you to the dwellings of those you visit. This work cannot be done by proxy. Money lent or given will not accomplish it. Sermons will not do it. *By visiting the people, talking, praying, sympathizing with them, you will win hearts"* (*Testimonies to the Church*, 9:40, 41).

May the Lord help us to use our best energies as we actively devise methods that will bring success in our efforts to reach the lost.

"Can I sing for you?"

Richard Gutierrez found Karen working on a flowerbed on her front lawn. As he tried to hand her a book, she shook her head. "I'm not interested. My back hurts, and I'm not in the mood today," she said.

Gutierrez asked if he could instead sing "Turn Your Eyes Upon Jesus" for her. Karen nodded. After he sang, he handed Karen a copy of *Peace Above the Storm* and told her that it held the keys to peace and freedom from worry. Karen began to weep, saying she needed that peace.

Then Karen surprised the young man. "You're in luck! I just withdrew five thousand dollars from the bank," Karen said, handing him a hundred-dollar donation. "Thank you so much! This book will be such a blessing."

Gutierrez said later that he recognized at that moment that God had arranged the meeting with Karen.

He told Karen that he would like to give her some more books right away.

"For that donation, you can have these other books as well," he said, holding out several devotional and health books.

Karen gave Gutierrez $200 and chose nineteen of his books. After he prayed for her, she signed up for Bible studies.

We are encouraged to "learn to sing the simplest of songs. These will help you in house-to-house labor, and hearts will be touched by the influence of the Holy Spirit" (*Evangelism,* 502). This became very real for Richard that day!

God's little bird

Shannon Parker was working as a leader, training a student named Mark Warren. They were not having very good success canvassing that day. At that particular moment they had just knocked on a door, and no one answered. They stopped in the driveway behind a truck to pray that God would lead them.

Partway into the prayer, they heard a man's voice say, "Can I help you?"

They looked up and saw a man coming from the backyard to see what they were doing. Shannon and Mark quickly pulled out books and began showing them to him. He seemed particularly interested in *Peace Above the Storm* and *He Taught Love,* yet he felt the need to pause their canvass and share with them that he was an alcoholic and was struggling. Badly, in fact. He went on to explain that he had just been in the backyard praying when they came! He was feeling really discouraged and was praying for God's guidance and power.

He said, "Though my eyes were closed in prayer, I had faintly heard a little bird hopping around continuously, flapping its wings and making noise while I prayed." When he looked up to see what the commotion was, he somehow saw Shannon and Mark through the front and back windows of his truck. And they were praying too!

The three ended up having a wonderful conversation and meaningful prayer together. He took *Peace Above the Storm* and *He Taught Love.* All three of them were completely amazed that God had sent that little bird to get his attention, and that Shannon and Mark were standing in exactly the right place for him to see them. Had they not stopped to pray at that moment, they would have missed meeting him! They were very thankful for that divine appointment and God's little bird.

Atheist trying out God meets canvasser

Sarah was a young woman that Andrew Innocent met, who was very interested in the *Seven Secrets* cookbook that he had introduced. He also canvassed her on *Peace Above the Storm* and *Man of Peace*, but she handed them back and said she wouldn't read them.

Andrew decided to simply close her on the cookbook alone. As she was writing the check for a high donation, he noticed her guitar. He asked if she was an instrumentalist, she said she was, and indicated that she played the guitar, French horn, piano, and sang as well.

When he heard her mention the piano, his ears perked up, as he played piano also.

He offered her an extra book for her large donation called *Your Pets and Your Health*, since she loved pets. Then he said he would play the piano for her as a thank-you.

Andrew played the song "Give Thanks," and Sarah began to sing along. She explained that after growing up in an atheist home, she had recently begun attending church to see if she could actually believe in something. That was how she had come to know the words to that song.

The Holy Spirit then began to strongly impress Andrew to leave her the book *Peace Above the Storm*, although she had already dismissed it. He felt the impression strongly but didn't know how to bring it up again without it seeming awkward. He stalled in leaving, waiting for God to show him what to do, and then finally just prayed with her and left.

He continued to canvass other homes, but the Lord kept telling him to go back and leave Sarah a copy of *Peace Above the Storm*. Finally Andrew gave in and went back and handed her the book, saying, "I really want you to read this!"

Sarah replied, "I'll read it, just for you."

"I know that book will change her life for the better," Andrew said. "Praise God for being persistent with me and softening her heart."

Music opens doors

The day was going great. Zuzana Metzova had found many people interested in her books, but a greater blessing was awaiting her late on that Sunday afternoon.

The special blessing came through meeting Peggy, who was very nice and engaging and had decided to get some books from Zuzana.

"Do you by any chance play the piano too?" Peggy inquired as they were wrapping things up.

"I love playing the piano!" Zuzana replied enthusiastically. In fact, she not only liked to play the piano, she loved to sing as well.

"You see, we have a church service this evening, but our pianist isn't available," Peggy told Zuzana. "Could you . . ." she questioned.

"I will check into it," Zuzana replied excitedly.

After clearing that request with her colporteur leader, Zuzana played the piano for the local Baptist church's song service, followed by a special music selection of one of her favorite songs, "People Need the Lord."

The church members were very appreciative of her willingness to help them at the last minute and for her sharing the message in song. At the end of their Sunday evening service, the Baptist pastor stood up to thank Zuzana for her ministry in song, made an appeal, and took up an offering to help further her Christian education. In exchange for the money donated, she left a set of books with the church for their library.

God has many ways to place His truth in the places that need it, and this time He did it through the ministry of music!

Sheep in other folds

Daniel Gomez walked into a business that was being canvassed by his friend, Natalie Cordova. He gently interrupted Natalie's canvass to ask if he could use the restroom. The woman smiled and pointed to the back of the business, where a man was seated in front of a computer. The man showed him to the restroom.

Daniel was about to leave the business, when Natalie turned to him and encouraged him to go and talk to the man in the back who had directed him to the restroom.

He went to the back of the store and once again found the man, apparently the owner of the business. After a short introduction, he began showing him some message books. As Daniel canvassed, the man didn't say much to clue Daniel in on his interest. All at once, he watched the owner stand up, walk out of the store with the books, and head to his pickup truck! He would be getting books! At the same time, Daniel noticed that the woman that Natalie was canvassing was also getting books.

Later, as Daniel was preparing to leave, he asked the owner if he could pray for him.

"Yes, pray for me," the man replied. "Pray that I may find a new church, one that keeps the Sabbath."

"Who told you about the Sabbath?" Daniel asked.

"My Bible told me about the Sabbath," the man answered.

He went on to tell Daniel that he had once been a pastor, but when he embraced the Sabbath truth and began preaching it, his denomination told him that if he continued to promote the Sabbath, he would be removed from office and from church membership.

He persisted, and in the end the denomination did as it had threatened. But this pastor was not discouraged. He told Daniel that he was currently acting as pastor for two groups that were keeping the Sabbath. All of them were praying that the Lord would lead them to a church that also kept the Sabbath.

Daniel was bubbling over with excitement as he shared with the man that he was a Seventh-day Adventist and that he, too, kept the seventh-day Sabbath!

The canvassing leader stayed in touch with the pastor, and he was connected with the local church.

Upon reflection, Daniel marveled that this man would walk away from a nice salary, a house, and a car that the church provided for him in order to follow the truth of the Bible.

John 10:16 says, "Other sheep I have which are not of this fold; them also I must bring, and they will hear My voice; and there will be one flock and one shepherd."

A storm after peace

Christopher Miller and his friends returned early from canvassing that day, because they had run out of books. They decided to restock their bags at the school and then canvass nearby for the last day of canvassing.

That day Chris met Mike. Mike was a happily married truck driver. He was in especially good spirits, because he had just gotten a new puppy to travel with him on the road. Chris showed Mike the books that he had and explained to him what he was doing. Mike, a devout Christian, was very interested in what he was doing and invited him inside. They had a good conversation, and then he handed Chris a check. He had given Chris four times the suggested donation for *Peace Above the Storm*! And as it turned out, that wouldn't be the last that Chris would see of Mike.

Seven months later, while passing out flyers for a community event hosted by two local Adventist churches, Chris found himself on a familiar street. He recognized that he was close to where Mike lived and decided pay him a visit and invite him to the event they were hosting.

As Mike came to the door, Chris saw that he wasn't the same man he had met seven months earlier. Chris reintroduced himself and asked if he remembered him. Mike replied that he did, but Chris could tell that something wasn't right. It seemed as though all the life and happiness in him had been sucked out.

Still wondering what was wrong, Chris continued and shared the reason for the return visit. He invited Mike to join them for the community social that was coming up.

Mike said he wouldn't be able to make it. When he asked Chris which church he was a member of, Chris gently replied that he was a Seventh-day Adventist Christian.

Mike seemed to relax a bit when he shared that, and continued, "I'm almost done with that book you gave me."

Switching back to the topic at hand, he continued, "I can't come to the social because I don't have transportation."

Chris acknowledged that, but wondered about the truck he used to have. That's when Mike opened up. "I don't have it anymore. Shortly after I met you, my wife left me, I lost my job, and I have to take medication because of an illness."

So the truck was sold to make ends meet, it seemed. Mike's voice was lifeless and his demeanor numb as he spoke those words to Chris that day.

117

Chris was speechless for a moment. Then God began bringing thoughts to his mind, and he tried to encourage Mike. He reminded him that God never leaves us, even when others do. Mike went inside to get his Bible as Chris continued with a promise from Psalm chapter 27.

Mike's spirit seemed to gradually lighten, and he told Chris that he was not depressed, even though his conditions were unfortunate. He shared with him that he had held on to the promise of peace that the Bible gave him.

He again reiterated, "I have been reading that book you gave me, and I'm almost done. That book, along with my Bible, has been keeping me going."

It seemed to Chris that Satan had been upset that Mike received that *Peace Above the Storm* and had tried to destroy his faith.

As they continued sharing, Chris echoed Mike's thoughts of God's power to uphold us through trial.

Before leaving, Chris offered to pray with Mike. He agreed to it, and after the prayer he seemed excited.

"I know you're from God!" he exclaimed. "The Holy Spirit is with us! Know how I can tell? Look here!" He extended his arms to show Chris his goose bumps.

Chris gave Mike a hug and left with a sense of the struggle that comes with making decisions for God, as well as a renewed confidence in the power of God to give peace beyond our circumstances.

Dare I enter?

Rena Lee paused in front of the door as she waited for a response to her knock. As so often happens, no one came. As she turned to leave, she heard voices coming from the backyard. Peering down the driveway, she saw three people talking together.

She hesitated on the front step and wondered, *Should I interrupt them or not? Maybe they'll think I am rude for intruding on them in their backyard.*

Whispering a short prayer, she marched up to them. After canvassing one of the people, the man smiled at her and said, "I read the Bible."

When she heard his accent, she realized that he was Portuguese and wondered how much of her canvass he had understood.

Rena decided to take a different approach and asked, "What church do you go to?"

In broken English he replied, "I used to go to an evangelical church."

He then asked her the same question.

"I am personally a Seventh-day Adventist Christian. Have you heard of us?" she asked.

Even though he smiled, his expression seemed to tell her that he hadn't.

He then decided to lead the conversation and asked her, "Why is it that so many Christians go to church on Sunday instead of Saturday?"

His question surprised her. She began to mentally formulate a response from all the texts and history she could recall. Rena shared with him about the change of the Sabbath and why Sunday is not the true day of worship.

After she finished, he nodded his head in agreement and said, "You know."

He continued, "I used to go to church on Sunday, but as I studied my Bible I realized it said Saturday that was the seventh-day Sabbath. When I asked my pastor why we go to church on Sunday, do you know what he said?"

Rena shrugged in response.

"He said it was because Jesus rose on Sunday." The man slowly shook his head and said adamantly, "In Genesis and Revelation it says the seventh day! I don't go to church anymore, but I do study the Bible and listen to messages on CD. I am looking for a church that keeps the seventh-day Sabbath."

As they continued their conversation, he spoke about last-day events and the pope's claimed authority over the Bible. Rena listened and thought to herself, *This man may not be a Seventh-day Adventist, but he sure speaks like one!*

She slipped *The Great Controversy* into his hand and pointed out that it covered the same topics they had been speaking about. He glanced at the pages as he flipped through.

"I can't read English very well, but I will try to read this, and I want to help you out."

As he went to get a donation for the book from inside his home, she called in to him, "Could I see those CDs you were talking about?"

He returned shortly with his neatly organized CDs. "Here they are!"

Rena looked at them and saw a little logo in the corner that she recognized—

three angels circling a globe. *They must be Seventh-day Adventist CDs,* she thought.

He pulled out his worn Portuguese Bible and flipped through its pages. She could see highlights and notes everywhere and was truly humbled. She realized that even though she was a student literature evangelist, this man was more dedicated to Bible study than she was.

A few weeks later, a young Portuguese-speaking Bible worker miraculously moved into the area. Rena's leader, Josiah, remembered where the home was and decided to introduce the Bible worker to her contact. The man wasn't home when they got there. Bruno, the Bible worker, went back again on another occasion, and that time found him home.

Bruno was able to start Bible studies with this man and his wife. In addition, the couple began visiting the church and a few weeks later were baptized!

Many times Rena had read and heard of amazing stories like this, but never expected to have such an experience herself while canvassing. After it happened, she was grateful to have been used as a tool for God and to have seen His hand in every step.

The child angel for the canvasser

Rebekah Ondrizek walked down the street feeling a bit discouraged. The neighborhood she was working in didn't seem very friendly. She prayed as she walked, finding comfort in knowing that her Savior was right there with her.

As Rebekah approached the next house, she could see several kids playing in the driveway. She wished she knew them better so that she could just play with them for a few minutes.

She walked up to the house, and the kids suddenly surrounded her, plying her with questions. "What's your name? Whatcha doing? What are those books about?"

Rebekah introduced herself, and they told her their names and what game she had interrupted by her presence. As soon as the game was mentioned, she was called upon to act as a duly impressed onlooker as one of the boys showed off some stunt he thought was cool. The laughter and smiles of the children were like sunbeams to Rebekah's discouraged heart. With a spring in her step that hadn't been there before, she completed her ascent to the door.

Before she could knock, however, one of the kids opened the door and shouted for the owner. A burly man came to the door, gruffly demanding to know why he'd been interrupted. "This is our new friend, Rebekah!" the kids announced. "She's a student, and she has books, and they've got pretty pictures!"

"Oh, well, I guess I'll take a look," the man grumbled, still trying to appear gruff and unfriendly. Though he very quickly handed the books back to her, he was much more friendly as he bid her good day.

Nine-year-old Piper, however, wasn't satisfied to let her go. "May I come with you and help you?" she pleaded.

Rebekah told her that if she got her mother's permission, she could walk with her a little way.

She skipped off to ask her mother as Rebekah made her way to the next door, waving goodbye to her new little friends as she left.

Before long, Piper came running up to her. "My mom said I can go with you up to our friend's house!" she happily announced. "I told Mama I wanted her to get your cookbook, but she said no, she didn't want it."

They made their way down the street, Piper chattering at every step. A fascinating series of events began to unfold.

Piper wanted to do everything for Rebekah. She wanted to knock on the door. She wanted to introduce her. She wanted to show the people the cookbook. If no one was home, she was delighted to leave a Bible study card on the door. She wanted to do everything!

This girl wasn't shy, either. Having spent all of her nine years in that neighborhood, she knew every house they stopped at. Sometimes, when someone wasn't coming to the door fast enough, Piper would open the door just a crack and shout to them to come, or else she'd pull Rebekah around to the back door to knock there. The people came grumbling, but as soon as they saw Piper, they'd break into smiles. She was the key to their hearts.

All too soon, they reached the house where Piper had to stop. Though she begged to go farther, Rebekah insisted on her returning to her mother. Before she left, though, Rebekah asked Piper which one of the children's books she would like.

With a smile, she chose *Prince of Peace*, the beautiful retelling of the life of Christ for kids.

With a wave of her hand, Piper skipped back to her friends, clutching her book to her chest as she ran.

Rebekah was reminded of Jesus' own words: " 'Let the little children come to Me, and do not forbid them; for of such is the kingdom of God.' And He took them up in His arms, laid His hands on them, and blessed them" (Mark 10:14, 16).

Another chance to get the books

It was the first time Dwight Blake's group had canvassed parking lots, and that day it happened to be a local department store parking lot.

A couple of days before, Dwight had canvassed a young man who was really interested in *The Great Controversy* and *Man of Peace*, but he had no money on him. Since he had no money, Dwight wasn't able to leave him a book, but he shared a Bible study card.

Then at the department store, Dwight had been canvassing the parking lot all day in the hot sun along with the other canvassers in his team, and they were glad to stop for a lunch break.

They had gone to a sub shop to buy sandwiches and were standing in line, when Dwight heard one of his fellow canvassers speaking to a man ahead of him in line. When he looked to his left, it was the same young man from the previous day who had wanted the books!

When the young man glanced Dwight's way, he recognized him also, made the connection, and said he was still interested in getting those books.

After getting his sandwich, the young man went to an ATM and drew out $40. He met them outside at their minivan, where he got *The Great Controversy*, *Man of Peace*, *God's Answers to Your Questions*, and *Peace Above the Storm*. The man was also quite interested in learning more about the Seventh-day Adventist Church, so Dwight gave him a card with an address for the local Adventist church. God really wanted him to have another chance to get those books!

Divine appointment at lunch

After a successful morning visiting businesses, Titus Morris and other canvassers were picked up and driven to a lunch spot.

Titus thought back on the morning's blessings: many divine appointments, heartfelt prayers with people, many copies of *Steps to Christ*, and nine larger books.

It had been an exhilarating and satisfying morning doing ministry!

Soon they arrived at a gas station that had a sub shop inside. When they were seated at the tables, halfway through their lunch break, a woman walked in and interrupted their conversation. She wanted to know if one of the guys would help move some bags of mulch from the storefront into the back of her van.

Shane and Titus jumped up and went out to lift the bags into the trunk. "Thank you, thank you!" she exclaimed. "Those bags were just too heavy for me to lift, and you fellows are a great help! I've been driving all day looking for mulch, and I finally found it. Here, take this," she gestured as she held out some money to them. "This is for helping me."

"No," Titus told her. "Jesus says, 'Inasmuch as ye have done it unto one of the least of these, my brethren, ye have done it unto me.' I actually helped Jesus today, and He has paid me way, way more than I could possibly deserve. So since Christ has, is, and will pay me, you don't need to."

Just then, Titus's friend Shane walked up and handed their new friend a *Steps to Christ*, which she gratefully accepted.

"I love Jesus too! Wow, this is so wonderful!" She gushed. "So what are you guys doing this summer?"

At that very moment Titus was thinking, *This is really neat, but this is lunch-time, and I want to finish eating.* He wouldn't dare tell her that, of course, so she continued prying him with good questions about the student literature ministry and sharing Jesus door to door with people.

Her excitement about Jesus prompted him into action, and Titus finally set aside his desire to finish his lunch right then. He would wait. "Hey, why don't you come over to the van with me, and I'll show you the books."

"Sure, I'd love to," she agreed. After looking through the books, she picked *He Taught Love*. As Titus shared with her how the book had brought him closer to Christ, she assured him that she would definitely read it too.

Pressing the donation for the book into his hand, she asked that he pray for her ministry, that God would use her and help her to show Jesus to others. As they each turned to go, she called out that she would pray for him as well.

Walking back over to his lunch, Titus realized the amazing blessing the two of them had just shared. God had timed their meeting perfectly by sending the group to eat there and sending her to buy mulch. As he ate the food that God had provided, He had sent Titus to share some spiritual food with one who was hungering for it.

Who could have set up such an amazing appointment? Was it just chance or incredible luck? No! Only God can arrange these meetings; only He can fill one's spiritual hunger. Our Savior will use you to save someone from spiritual starvation if you allow Him!

9

The Invisible Helper

"The king's heart is in the hand of the LORD, like the rivers of water;
He turns it wherever He wishes" (Prov. 21:1).

In working for Christ, we should always keep in mind that it is His work and not ours, and He is continually preparing the way for its success through the Holy Spirit.

When Joshua sent spies into Jericho, they were received by Rahab the harlot, who said to them, "The terror of you has fallen on us, and that all the inhabitants of the land are fainthearted because of you. For we have heard how the LORD dried up the water of the Red Sea for you when you came out of Egypt" (Joshua 2:9, 10). As early as forty years beforehand, the Lord had prepared the way for victory.

When King Nebuchadnezzar of ancient Babylon allowed his pride to keep him from yielding to the influence of the Holy Spirit, the Lord brought about a change in the circumstances of Nebuchadnezzar's life that prepared the king's heart for the reception of truth.

When God wanted to reach the jailer at Philippi and all of his household with the gospel, He allowed a chain of events to unfold that led the jailer to cry out, " 'Sirs, what must I do to be saved?' " (Acts 16:30).

And in our day, Jesus is still preparing the way before His servants so that people will be open to receive and embrace the truth. We are told that "there is far more being done by the universe of Heaven than we have any idea of, in preparing the way so that souls shall be converted" (*Evangelism*, 127). The precious promise is given, "Under divine guidance, go forward in the work, and look to the Lord for aid. The Holy Spirit will attend you. Angels of heaven will accompany you, preparing the way" (*Colporteur Ministry*, 22).

May the Lord help us to labor in His strength, trusting in His ability to prepare hearts to receive Him.

The ripple effect

Literature evangelists Maverick Khongphan and Amber Cotrone were going door to door on a rainy Sunday. They didn't realize it then, but their work that day was the start of a fruitful ripple effect for God's kingdom.

That day, Maverick and Amber met a young girl named Jennifer, who told them she was an agnostic. "My grandparents are Baptists, and they are constantly trying to get me to go to church with them, but I guess I'm just a need-to-see-it-to-believe-it kind of girl," Jennifer explained. "And I just never felt like God was real."

Nevertheless, as they continued getting to know each other, Amber offered Jennifer Bible studies. Jennifer quickly said no. Maverick then invited her to an evangelistic series in their area. "There'll be free food!" he told her with a grin.

"Oh, but I'm vegan," Jennifer protested.

"That's great!" Maverick replied happily. "It's a vegetarian potluck!"

Jennifer was stunned. "Oh. Well. I'll think about it," she responded. Then Jennifer started to have a strange feeling that she needed to change her mind about the Bible studies as well. She didn't realize it at that moment, but she's now confident that the Holy Spirit was working on her heart. By the Holy Spirit's influence, Jennifer did change her mind—she signed up for Bible studies and committed to attending the evangelistic series.

Jennifer attended the entire series and spent the next two months studying the

Bible with Amber. At the end of the two months, Jennifer decided to be baptized! But her decision was only just the first ripple.

A year later, Jennifer decided to become a literature evangelist herself. She joined a student program in her area and began learning how to knock on doors. Of her experience, she reports, "It is definitely a huge blessing. I have learned so much. It has been very character building. It has shown me how to trust in God more."

As she worked door to door, Jennifer herself began to have experiences where she could see the Holy Spirit working to change lives. The change in her life was now leading to changes in the lives of others. Jennifer is a living example of this powerful statement: "Let canvassers go forth with the word of the Lord. . . . One soul truly converted will bring others to Christ. Thus the work will advance into new territory" (*Testimonies for the Church,* 6:315).

Our prayer should be that we are the one soul that is truly converted and leading others to Jesus. Who can tell where the ripple effect of our labor will stop?

The personal touch

Mark Smith, a student literature evangelist, met a woman named Sandie and shared some health-related books with her. Everything was going well until he pulled out a *Bible Readings for the Home*.

"I don't believe in God!" Sandie exclaimed angrily. "If God is so good, why did he allow me to get raped when I was a child? Why did he allow my husband to leave me for another woman? Why did he allow social services to take away my kids? Why is my life a living hell?" Sandie continued venting for some time, using very descriptive language. She was hurting, and Mark didn't know what to say. Helplessly, he silently pleaded with God for help.

"Sandie, I don't know why you were abused as a child. I don't understand why your husband left you or why they took your children away. There are many things I don't understand, but there is something I know for sure. I came here to meet you this summer, to let you know that God loves you and He just wants you to come home," Mark said.

Hearing those words, Sandie broke into sobs. Through Mark, she came face to face with the compassionate, personal touch of God. Needless to say, she took the book and signed up for Bible Studies.

Crystal, another student literature evangelist, knocked on Tony's door but was met with an angry rejection. She felt the man needed something, so she left a pamphlet version of *Steps to Christ* on the windshield of his car. Having gone a few houses down the street, she saw Tony running toward her. He was mad!

"I told you I wasn't interested!" he shouted at Crystal. "Why did you leave this book on my windshield?" He then started to swear. Tony railed on for some time before he finally paused long enough to take a breath.

"I'm sorry, sir," Crystal apologized, tears in her eyes. "I saw that you were having a stressful day, and I just wanted to leave a little peace in your life."

Tony was quiet for a moment, and then he invited Crystal back to the house. He opened the door and told her to look inside.

"What do you see?" he asked.

Crystal peered inside. There was nothing inside—no furniture or personal belongings at all. "It's empty!" she exclaimed.

"Yes, totally empty," Tony agreed. There were tears in his eyes as he explained that he had just returned from a trip to find that his wife had left him and taken everything in the house with her. "But what else do you have in that bag?"

Tony ended up getting all of Crystal's books and signing up for Bible studies. But it was Crystal's prayer for him that led Tony to the foot of the cross.

It is true that life is full of trials, as both Sandie and Tony experienced. Everyone has them, regardless of their relationship to God. However, the difference is that God's children know where to find hope and comfort. They know God's promise that while "weeping may endure for a night . . . joy comes in the morning" (Psalm 30:5). And not only do they know it for themselves, but they can reach out to share that comfort with others.

Dear God, please send an Adventist

Pat became a Seventh-day Adventist when she lived on the east coast of America, in her teenage years. Through a series of unfortunate events, Pat stopped going to church and planned never to return. Some years later, Pat moved to the opposite coast. After sixty years and ten kids, Pat began to feel that she needed something more.

One day, Pat was in her home when she felt something tell her that she should go into her garage and look for a box of books. The books were leftovers from her church-going days—books about the Sabbath and the Adventist faith. Though she resisted for a while, eventually she gave in and went out to her garage. To her surprise, the books were in the very first box she looked in!

As Pat began to read the books, she was convicted that she should start keeping the Sabbath again. She did, along with her daughter Cathy. After so many years away from her faith, she wasn't sure how to keep the Sabbath anymore. So, she did the only thing she knew to do: she prayed that God would send a Seventh-day Adventist to her door if God really wanted her to get back into church. Two months later, Irene Monterroso, a student literature evangelist, knocked on her door.

When Pat found out that Irene was with the Adventist Church, she was ecstatic. "Can you have someone give me Bible studies?" she asked eagerly.

Irene took Pat's contact information and connected her with Joel Moutray, a local Bible worker. Joel began meeting with Pat and Cathy twice a week. When he gave Pat a copy of *The Great Controversy*, she finished it in a week. When the church hosted an evangelistic series, Pat and Cathy attended every single night. They were both baptized and are now active members of their local church.

Many times, the work of the literature evangelist is a silent work—hearts are touched and lives are changed long after the student leaves the door. But other times, God allows us to see our role in His work of saving souls. Jeremiah records a beautiful statement: "The Lord has appeared of old to me, saying: 'Yes, I have loved you with an everlasting love; therefore with lovingkindness I have drawn you' " (Jeremiah 31:3). How many others like Pat are being drawn with God's everlasting love? How many others like Pat are just waiting for someone to point them in the right direction? If we never step out in faith to find them, we'll never know.

God knows the way

The neighborhood Rebekah Ondrizek was working was obviously a rich one. The people in the first few houses weren't really interested in the books, though several of them gave small donations. She walked along with a smile and a song, encouraged as she remembered the Spanish-speaking waitress and her employer that she'd met earlier that day, both of whom had been delighted with the Spanish editions of *The Great Controversy* and *Peace Above the Storm*.

At the next house, as soon as Rebekah introduced herself to the man inside, she could tell that this was not the typical rich, need-nothing family. The man called to his wife, and together they told Rebekah about their kids and asked her about her education and the scholarship program. As she began to show them the books, their friendliness changed to subdued excitement. Rebekah could hear in the woman's voice an intense longing for the salvation of her children and a deep love of Christ. Her husband, though showing less emotion, still made it obvious that he shared his wife's love for the Lord and her desire for their kids to love Him too.

Within moments, all of Rebekah's books were on their table. The couple couldn't decide which book to look at next, finding each of them fascinating. Rebekah handed the woman *The Ministry of Healing*, explaining that this book contained the blueprint for a happy, Christ-centered home. The woman's eyes lit up, and she snatched the book out of Rebekah's hands.

"Honey!" she exclaimed, "This is just the book we need! Will you read it with me?"

"Darling," he replied, "you know I'm not a reader . . . but, I'll gladly listen if you read it to me!"

"We'll start it tonight!" his wife declared. She also chose a DVD on Daniel 9 called *The Ultimate Timeline*.

As the woman went into the other room to get her purse, Rebekah overheard her speaking to her husband: "Maybe she's an angel, honey! I think she just might be." When the couple came back, the woman told Rebekah she knew she'd been sent to them that day.

"And, I have to ask you something," she said with a smile. "Are you an angel?"

"Oh, no!" Rebekah assured her, "I'm no angel! But I work with them!"

Rebekah prayed with the couple and moved on down the street. A few doors down, she met a neighbor who wasn't too sure she could trust the scholarship program, wondering if it was a scam. Just as she was about to return the books and close the door, Rebekah heard her name being called. Turning toward the street, she saw the woman she'd just met, riding her bike and waving.

"Rebekah! God bless you, friend!" the woman called.

Rebekah smiled and waved back, grateful for the kindness, as it took the sting out of the rejection she was expecting. But as she turned back to the door, the neighbor's suspicious expression had changed to a smile.

"May I see those children's books again?" she asked. "I think my grandson would like one!" As she pulled a donation from her purse, she commented, "I sure like our neighbor! She has the sweetest family."

Rebekah couldn't help but agree. Later, she reflected that God "knows the way to open doors, both literal ones and figurative ones." And isn't it encouraging that the One who knows how to the open doors is also responsible for the results? "But when we give ourselves wholly to God and in our work follow His directions, He makes Himself responsible for its accomplishment. . . . Not once should we even think of failure. We are to co-operate with One who knows no failure" (*Christ's Object Lessons,* 363).

The man of the house

In the summer of 2005, Sebastien Braxton was going door to door, making appointments to show families larger sets of books, including the Conflict of the Ages series and the Bible Story set. At one particularly beautiful house, he met a mother with three daughters. Her interest was strong, but instead of showing her the books right away, Sebastien insisted on a time when both she and her husband could be present.

That evening, at the agreed-upon time, Sebastien returned. The man of the house welcomed him in and spent time telling him about how he owned his own business and had built his home himself—including the backyard swimming pool.

As Sebastien displayed the Bible Story set, the wife had to jump up frequently to attend to things in the kitchen. Her husband was able to sit and listen carefully and, by the end of the presentation, was clearly convicted.

As Sebastien made his closing appeal, the man turned to his wife. "These books would be such a blessing to our family, don't you think, dear?" he remarked.

"Perhaps," the wife responded, sounding unconvinced. She then brought up several objections about information she'd missed on her trips in and out of the room. Sebastien patiently repeated the information, but to little avail.

"They're just too pricey, in my opinion," she said. "And really, I don't think they're that useful."

"Golf is pricey and not that useful," her husband responded. "And I spend plenty on that. Go get the checkbook."

The wife left in a huff but returned with the checkbook as requested. Taking the checkbook from his wife, the husband invited Sebastien into his study. As they sat down, the man began to confide in Sebastien.

"Sebastien, as soon as you finished your presentation, I knew that God sent you here. You see, another family has been taking my girls to church every weekend. I come home from work, ready to see them, and they're gone! I ask my wife, and she says the neighbor family took them to church and to lunch. I was OK with that for a while, but then I realized that some other man was leading my daughters spiritually! I wanted to take back that role in my daughters' lives, but, until you came, I just didn't know how."

As the man continued, Sebastien watched tears fill his eyes and overflow down his cheeks. "With these books, I know that I'll have the opportunity to talk to my girls about God and His word. I thank God for sending you to my home! He has used you to help me be the man in my family that He wants me to be," the man said. "Will you please pray for me? And ask God to bless my home?"

Sebastien was happy to oblige, and his heart was light as he left that evening. We are promised that when parents "consecrate themselves wholly to God," that "the Lord will devise ways and means whereby a transformation may take place in their household" (*Child Guidance*, 172). In this case, God had known in advance which spouse needed to hear Sebastien's presentation the most and arranged the evening accordingly.

United in love

As Delon Lawrence approached a house, a barking dog darted out of the bushes and straight toward him. Delon stopped right in his tracks and began to pray.

The next three minutes seemed like forever to Delon, but eventually the front door opened—and two additional dogs joined the first! Delon stood his ground, still praying. Eventually, the dogs' owner came out to greet him, and when he did, the dogs relaxed.

Delon was certain that, after that kind of reception, this must be a divine appointment. He started his presentation with the book, *God's Answers to Your Questions*.

"I'm an atheist," the man said, interrupting Delon.

"Oh? Why are you an atheist?" Delon asked, unperturbed.

The man looked surprised at Delon's cool response, but he invited Delon inside.

They sat opposite each other at the dining table and were soon joined by the man's wife, who described herself as an agnostic.

The man started to explain his beliefs to Delon, starting with evolution and the many problems religion has caused. Delon listened carefully, without interruption, even though he strongly disagreed on many points. When the man finished, Delon spoke up.

"Our beliefs are vastly different when it comes to the origin of man and religion," Delon admitted, "but we're really just the same—we both need love in our life. And I know God exists because His love is perfectly evident in my life." The man listened intently as Delon shared how God's love had worked in his life, but then he was still insistent that God couldn't exist. However, after hearing Delon's story, the wife seemed more open.

Eventually, the man went upstairs and returned with a twenty-dollar donation for Delon's education. Delon begged him to take a few of his books, but he refused.

"Hey, I have a question," the man's wife interjected. "What about people who don't know Jesus' name, but they live good lives? What happens to them?"

"Salvation isn't just about knowing Jesus' name, like some magic trick," Delon explained. "What saves us is accepting His grace. Then, by His power, we can live in His character."

Something about Delon's words took the couple by surprise, and the man had a change of heart about the books.

"Well, perhaps we'll take those two books after all," he said, reaching out for *The Great Controversy* and *Man of Peace*.

When Delon's leader came to pick him up, he was still talking to them. The couple was so kind and joyful that his leader thought they were Christians. As they were starting to pull away, the wife called out, saying, "May God be with you!"

Her husband said, "You will prosper since you are serving the Lord."

How much was accomplished through the listening ear and personal testimony of a young believer! Later, Delon reflected, "Arguing and disagreeing with non-believers avails nothing! First Corinthians 13:13 puts it the best: 'And now abide faith, hope, love, these three; but the greatest of these is love.' That's why we should avoid focusing on the differences that separate us and focus on the love of God that brings us together."

He will save His people

Dana Connell and her friend Maile Hoffman were working toward each other on their last street of the evening. When they met in the middle, the girls decided to go together to talk to a group of men standing at the end of the street. One man was selling rosaries to passersby, and there were a handful of small children running around them.

Maile talked to one man, who asked her to pray for his sister. The sister was being charged with murder, and her sentencing hearing was approaching. Maile promised that she would.

The man with the rosaries, hoping to make his own sale, interjected, telling the girls that he had rosaries for all kinds of prayers.

"No, thank you," Dana replied. "I talk to God as a friend."

"Me too!" a third man chimed in.

Dana turned toward the third man and pulled out a few books to show him. As the man realized the spiritual nature of her material, he looked up at the sky and said, "I hear You! I know You are trying to talk to me!" Turning back to Dana, he explained. "You are the third person to speak to me about God recently. He is trying to get my attention!"

"Yes, it sounds like God is indeed trying to talk to you!" Dana agreed. "What's your name?"

"Tito. Well, that's what people call me. But my real name is Jesus," Tito said, using the Spanish pronunciation.

"God definitely has great plans for your life, Tito . . . especially with a name like that!" Dana told the man. "Do you know what your name means?"

The question seemed strange to Tito. "What it means? You mean, other than the fact that it was Jesus' name too?"

"Yes! In the Bible, God's names are often descriptors of what God does. Jesus means 'He will save His people from their sins.' And His other name, Immanuel, means 'God with us.' In the Old Testament, one of God's names was 'Jehovah-Jireh,' which means 'My God provides.' "

Tito nodded, taking it all in. Then he began to share about his past—how he grew up in foster care, and went to church when he lived in New York, but since moving to his current city, he had fallen away from church.

"But God is definitely trying to talk to me now!" he said. "I just wish I could live up to my name."

Dana shook her head. "My friend, you can't! Jesus is the only one who can live up to a name that means 'He will save His people from their sins.' That's why Jesus came in the first place!"

Dana asked if she could pray for him, and Tito agreed. After her prayer, he pulled out the few dollars he had with him to give to Dana. In return, she handed him a pamphlet version of *Steps to Christ* and a door hanger advertising the Hope Channel on DIRECTV.

"Hey! I've got DIRECTV," Tito told Dana.

"You do? Then you should really watch this channel," Dana encouraged. "It can help you get to know the first Jesus."

"You know what? I will," Tito promised.

In the first century, when Joseph heard the words of the angel promising that his betrothed would have a son, he had only the beginning of an idea of what that Child would mean to the world. Yet he obeyed the angel's instructions: "You shall call His name JESUS, for He will save His people from their sins" (Matthew 1:21). Today, we not only have the privilege of experiencing Jesus' salvation ourselves, but also of introducing Him to others.

Comforted by God

Jonathan Zita met an elderly woman at her home as he was working door to door. At first, she refused anything he offered her, telling Jonathan she couldn't help him because her husband had passed away.

"That's OK," Jonathan said. Seeing her distress and wanting to help, he pulled a *Peace Above the Storm* from his bag as he continued. "I'm so sorry for your loss. May I give you this as a gift?"

As the woman accepted the beautiful, picture-filled *Peace Above the Storm*, tears welled up in her eyes and spilled onto her face.

"I'm sorry," she said through the tears. "My husband . . . he was so loving and so kind. But he wasn't just a good person. He was a wonderful Christian, too. I'm sorry. I'm not usually so emotional. It's been six months since he died, and . . ." Her voice trailed off.

Jonathan could see that her own lack of composure surprised her, and he spent the next few minutes just listening as she talked. After a while, the woman wiped her cheeks, straightened up, and said, "Well. I'd like to help you out. Wait here, won't you?"

She returned with a ten-dollar donation—exactly the amount Jonathan needed to cover the book. Before he left, Jonathan prayed for her. Taking her hand, he prayed that her home would still be a place of love, joy, and peace, and that the Holy Spirit would comfort her in her loss and help her to look forward to the great resurrection that would unite her with her husband again. Then he released her hand and, with a wave and a goodbye, was on his way to the next home.

Paul instructs us that God "comforts us in all our tribulation," so that "we may be able to comfort those who are in any trouble, with the comfort with which we ourselves are comforted by God" (2 Corinthians 1:4). It is often the colporteur's privilege to extend God's comfort to the hurting around them!

The ultimatum

As Edwin Zapata approached a home, he heard loud shouting and screaming coming from inside. There was clearly an argument underway. Before he knocked, Edwin bowed his head briefly, praying for the people inside.

At that moment, the door was flung open. Seeing Edwin, the man stopped abruptly. "What do you want?" he asked roughly.

Knowing he might not have much time, Edwin immediately handed the man a copy of *Peace Above the Storm*. Once the book was in the man's hand, Edwin introduced himself.

Almost instantly, the man's expression changed. He opened the screen door, sat down on the porch, and began to pour out his story.

"We believe in the same God," he said, "but God doesn't love me." The man, Dan, told how his wife had left him and how everything in his life seemed to be falling apart. "I just don't see God in what's happening!" he told Edwin. "How can a God of infinite love allow things like this to happen to His children? All I can think is that He must not love me. What do I have to do to obtain His favor?"

Edwin listened for a long time and encouraged Dan when he could. As their conversation neared its end, Dan shared that he was ready to give up on God altogether.

"I need answers, Edwin! I've decided to put God to the test. If, in four days, He doesn't speak to me, I'm giving up on Him," Dan said.

"Dan, you need this book. God can speak to you through this book! I know from personal experience!" Edwin insisted.

"All right," Dan agreed. "I'll get it." He went back inside and returned with an assortment of dollar bills and coins. "This is all I could find," he said.

Edwin was happy to give Dan the book for any amount, and as he left, he felt sure that God would answer Dan's plea through the simple yet profound message in the book he'd left behind. After all, as Jesus Himself promised, " 'Blessed are those who hunger and thirst for righteousness, for they shall be filled' " (Matthew 5:6).

A shining face

"What church do you go to?" Sheela Nadarajan asked a woman at the door, in an effort to start a conversation and make friends. It was a question Sheela asked routinely, but the woman's answer was extraordinary.

"I don't go to a church," Jane said. "But actually, I've been thinking about attending the Seventh-day Adventist church."

"Really?" Sheela exclaimed, shocked. "I'm a Seventh-day Adventist!"

Now it was Jane's turn to be surprised. "Wow, that's great! I thought only Mormons and Jehovah's Witnesses went door to door."

After Sheela showed Jane all of her materials, Jane said, "You know, I have to tell you something. Just before I opened the door, I looked through my window and saw that your face was lighted up and shining. You seemed so happy, and it made me want what you have. I knew there was something different about you. And I just can't believe that a Seventh-day Adventist came to my door! You are an answer to my prayer. I had been praying that someone would come and talk to me about religious things. And the shine on your face is great!"

As Jane gave a donation for four of Sheela's religious books, Sheela finally had the presence of mind to ask how it was that Jane knew about Adventists.

"Oh, I've known about them for a long time," Jane answered vaguely. "I've been curious about them, and I've been reading my Bible. And it seems that what they believe is right!"

Jane accepted the Bible studies that Sheela offered, and Sheela told her of another Adventist family that lived nearby. After praying together, Sheela continued on her way, not expecting to see Jane again.

When her leader heard about the experience, he suggested that they end their evening by returning to Jane's house and singing for her. So, that evening, a group of seven literature evangelists sang God's praises at Jane's door.

But the best part was still to come. Just three days later, on Sabbath morning, Jane came to the local Adventist church!

"I'm just amazed," Jane reported that first Sabbath, "that young people today could be so vibrant and on fire for the Lord, singing and working for Him!"

Exodus 34 records how Moses' face would shine whenever he met with God. In fact, it shone so brightly that the Israelites were afraid of him! Moses took to wearing a veil over his face, but he would always take the veil off when he went to talk with God. Referring to Moses' veil, Paul records that we also have the privilege of being transformed into God's shining glory: "But we all, with unveiled face, beholding as in a mirror the glory of the Lord, are being transformed into the same image from glory to glory, just as by the Spirit of the Lord" (2 Corinthians 3:18). And who can tell just how the Holy Spirit will make use of our shining faces for God's cause?

Turning curses to blessings

Early one morning, as Delaina Williams spent time in personal prayer and Bible study, she asked God for a special favor. "Lord," she prayed, "would You please do something amazing for me?"

Delaina didn't have to wait very long for God to answer her prayer. Later that day, as she was working a strip of businesses, she met the owner of a small shop. The woman treated her rudely and told her to leave. Swallowing her hurt feelings, Delaina responded with kindness. Smiling sincerely, she handed the woman a small Christian tract and said, "God bless you." Then she did as the woman had demanded and left the shop.

Two hours later, Delaina was making her way through the businesses on the opposite side of the street when she heard someone shouting.

"Miss, miss! Please come!"

Turning, Delaina saw the woman who had been rude to her. *Oh, great,* she thought uneasily. *What could she possibly want?* But, since she had been called, she made up her mind to go. She waited for a break in traffic and then crossed the street to the woman's shop.

As soon as she was within hearing range, the woman started apologizing. "I'm so sorry," she said in a rush. "I shouldn't have treated you that way. And how you treated me in return—your kind spirit and the little tract you left—well, it touched my heart. I prayed that God would bring you back to me so I could make things right."

Delaina and the woman talked for a long time that afternoon, and the woman asked Delaina to promise two things: first, that she would be successful, and second, that she would remain close to God. Then, with a smile, she opened the register and pulled out $140.

"Today is your lucky day," she told the astounded Delaina.

In return for her donation, the woman accepted several of Delaina's spiritual books, and Delaina went her way rejoicing over the change in heart she had just witnessed. "My faith in God was strengthened as I saw God do the impossible!" she wrote later.

It's true! Sometimes God turns curses into blessings when we follow the advice Paul gave the church in Rome: "Bless those who persecute you; bless and do not curse." "Do not be overcome by evil, but overcome evil with good" (Romans 12:14, 21).

10

His Faithfulness

"For as the rain comes down, and the snow from heaven, and do not return there, but water the earth, and make it bring forth and bud, that it may give seed to the sower and bread to the eater, so shall My word be that goes forth from My mouth; it shall not return to Me void, but it shall accomplish what I please, and it shall prosper in the thing for which I sent it" (Isaiah 55:10, 11).

The apostle Paul had long looked forward to the opportunity to preach the gospel at Rome. He envisioned the throngs of people coming to hear the gospel as he preached in this center of influence. His arrival at Rome, however, was very different from what he had at first imagined. Instead of being free to preach to the masses, he was being marched toward Rome chained hand and foot between some of the hardest looking criminals he had ever seen. It seemed that his hopes to win many souls to the truth were destined for disappointment.

When they reached Appii Forum, forty miles from Rome, the company made their way through the throngs of people. Paul sees the scornful looks directed his way and hears the mocking insults. What kind of influence can he possibly have now?

"Suddenly a cry of joy is heard, and a man springs from the passing throng and falls upon the prisoner's neck, embracing him with tears and rejoicing, as a son would welcome a long-absent father. Again and again is the scene repeated as . . . many discern in the chained captive the one who at Corinth, at Philippi, at Ephesus, had spoken to them the words of life. . . . They assure Paul that they have not forgotten him nor ceased to love him; that they are indebted to him for the joyful hope which animates their lives and gives them peace toward God. . . . In the midst of the weeping, sympathizing company of believers, who were not ashamed of his bonds, the apostle praised God aloud. The cloud of sadness that had rested upon his spirit was swept away. His Christian life had been a succession of trials, sufferings, and disappointments, but in that hour he felt abundantly repaid" (*The Acts of the Apostles*, 448, 449).

How often we get discouraged when we don't see the results we *think* we should, *when* we think we should see them! *Yet God is supremely faithful.* His word will not return void. Success will come in His way and His time. Souls will inherit the eternal kingdom through our feeble efforts because *He is faithful.* We are assured, "When we give ourselves wholly to God and in our work follow His directions, He makes Himself responsible for its accomplishment. He would not have us conjecture as to the success of our honest endeavors. Not once should we even think of failure. We are to co-operate with One who knows no failure" (*Christ's Object Lessons*, 363). "We are to work and pray, putting our trust in Him who will never fail" (*Testimonies to the Church*, 6:340). May our hearts forever resound with the refrain, "Great is Thy faithfulness"!

A wet, dusty answer

The Lord finds delight in strengthening our faith. Even if our faith is as little as a grain of mustard seed, when it takes hold of the power and the consistency of the Word of God—just like the true seed takes hold of the nutrients from the earth—it will move mountains.

While leading a canvassing program, Stefani Herrera found herself having an Elijah experience. Hurricane warnings were all over the news. Dread swept across the whole area. Besides knowing what kind of devastating blows it could bring, her little team of canvassers knew that the hurricane would also dramatically affect their canvassing work. Trusting in God, the team knelt down and prayed.

News spread that a wind could possibly slow down the hurricane's power. Remembering that a little cloud was what prompted Elijah to be assured that God would send a lot of rain as an answer to his persistent prayers, all fervently prayed that this little wind would destroy the hurricane altogether.

"Lord, please, if it is Your will, re-direct or stop the hurricane from coming here," they pleaded.

God answered; that powerful hurricane weakened to a tropical storm.

The news of a tropical storm was indeed an answer to prayer; nevertheless this storm was still troublesome to the team's canvassing experience. The weather forecast was for heavy rain and thunderstorms to hit that area right before the time they would start canvassing. Again, they prayed and moved forward in faith.

Upon their heading to the territory, the rain stopped! When the team took a break for lunch, the rain started pouring so furiously that by the time they walked from the van to the restaurant, each person was soaked. Again they prayed for the rain to stop, but it didn't. The forecast said it was to continue through to the next day.

After lunch it was cold, and the rain was still heavy. To escape the rain the team rushed into the vehicle. As they rushed, one of the canvassers reached over to open the driver's door from the inside, accidentally hitting the fire extinguisher and covering Stefani and all of books in the stock box in white spray. Now wet, cold, and dusty, with dusty white books and no good news in regard to the rain stopping, Stefani wondered what she should do as a leader.

They prayed. As they prayed, Stefani asked for guidance. She also asked that as God parted the Red Sea for the children of Israel once their feet were wet, that He might do the same for their team. After the prayer, she drove them to a different territory closer to the church that was filled with apartments. About thirty minutes after drop-off, the Lord answered the prayer and stopped the rain.

Even after the rain stopped, Stefani kept questioning her move. In the new territory, fewer books were going out. Had God really led her there? Had she only moved out of her fear that the rain might not stop?

When doubts come, by faith we need to take hold of God's promises; it is then that we can move mountains.

During Sabbath school that weekend, a young woman came to visit the church. One of the team members had canvassed her at the apartments and had invited her to church. She had a wonderful visit, and she and Stefani continued to keep in touch.

Looking back at the experience, Stefani realized that the Lord had worked everything out yet again, as an answer to prayer. Just before lunch that day she had prayed, "Lord, since many books are going out, it seems as if I should stay here. If you don't want me to come back, even though I don't know how, please show me." And sure enough, in a wet, cold and dusty way, the Lord answered by leading her to a place where they found the soul who was searching.

The moment of surrender

It was the middle of the summer colporteur program. Erdal Pascu was selling big books, the hardcover books like *Uncle Arthur's Bedtime Stories* and the Conflict of the Ages series. Unfortunately, her car was not running well. The windows couldn't be raised or lowered without blowing a fuse; and the air conditioning wasn't running either. So far Erdal had only had two sales, and one of them had cancelled. She started feeling like a leech, not bringing any money to the program yet using the program's resources.

One particular morning during worship, one of the other students spoke about a picture in *The Desire of Ages* that they all used frequently during their canvass for the Conflict of the Ages series. It was the picture of Jesus kneeling in the garden of Gethsemane. This friend encouraged the group to stop and really take in what that picture represents. It showed Jesus surrendering His life in spite of the fact that He had no guarantee that His great sacrifice would yield any results. At that moment He did not know for certain that any of us would be saved. Yet He gave up His life so that we might have a chance to have eternal life.

Later that evening Erdal was trying to find her way to the house where she was staying. She was hot and lost, as usual. Discouragement crept in more and more as she drove through town, sweating, with a map and her very poor sense of direction. *Maybe I should just go home.* Erdal sighed. She wasn't contributing anything to the program or to her scholarship.

Just then, that picture of Jesus in the garden popped into her mind. Immediately she remembered the worship from the morning, particularly that Christ went to the cross and surrendered His life for us there in the garden, with no guarantee that we would accept His sacrifice. Then a question came to her mind. "Erdal, will you work for Me this summer even if you get no more sales the rest of this summer?"

With teary eyes she thought, *How can I say no?* Right there she quietly surrendered to God the rest of her summer, her scholarship, and the shame of not contributing to the program's finances. The next day, as if God were rewarding her faithfulness, Erdal sold all the big books they carried, the largest number of books anyone sold at one house that summer!

The following day Erdal's lack of faith and fear took hold again, and she thought, *Well that's great that I got that big sale yesterday, but how long will it be until my next sale?* As if to rebuke her, that day God blessed her with her first sale of the Conflict of the Ages series. By the end of that week she had tripled her sales for the summer. God blessed the rest of that summer more than she expected.

The last door

It was Cassie Dhole's last door for the evening. Two women were sitting on the lawn enjoying a chat.

"No tengo dinero," they called out just as Cassie started walking toward them.

Cassie wasn't going to quit on them that easily. She struck up a little conversation with Rosy, the homeowner, and Leticia, her friend who was visiting. They began to make friends over *Peace Above the Storm* in Spanish.

"Could I see that book?" Leticia held out her hand.

After perusing it for a few moments, she asked if there were more books.

"Yes!" responded Cassie, handing her the cookbook, since the woman had already mentioned that she liked to cook. She already seemed quite interested in it.

"Do you have any grandchildren?" asked Cassie.

"Yes, I do."

Pulling a couple more out of her stack, Cassie showed her *Storytime* and *Prince of Peace*, excellent children's books. These Leticia liked as well, and she decided to fetch the money to get them. As she walked to her home two doors down, Cassie had one more opportunity to speak with Rosy, the homeowner. During their conversation, Cassie found out that Rosy had been a widow for about a year, and she was deeply depressed.

"Ma'am, *Peace Above the Storm* is exactly what you need."

"Really?" she asked.

"Yes," Cassie responded, "just trust me."

"I think you're right. I will get this book."

While Rosy went inside to get money, her friend came back with hers. Leticia ended up explaining that she was also Seventh-day Adventist, and once she saw who published the books, she knew that Cassie was a colporteur. She then promised at Cassie's request to share more books with Rosy. In the end, Leticia kept the cookbook, *Ancient Dream* DVD, and *Magic Kingdom* DVD, and Rosy ended up getting *Peace Above the Storm* to help her with her depression.

Slaying giants

One summer God had been convicting Jennita Schmidt to go higher in her commitment to canvassing and overcome her fears so that she could be more effective. He had been slaying many giants in the canvassing field as well as in her own heart.

The group leader had just dropped Jennita off in a huge plaza. It was tempting to fall back on old habits of walking in, asking for the manager, then canvassing the parking lot, but another student was working the parking lot, so the businesses were all she had.

While walking into a grocery store, Jennita prayed, "Lord, give me boldness and courage so that You can do something beyond what I expect."

She walked to the back of the store and began canvassing the department managers. Through one aisle on her route, Jennita canvassed an employee who almost immediately got *Peace Above the Storm*. This seemed to be God's sign that she needed to stay there as long as possible.

Jennita then went to the pharmacy department and canvassed the manager. When he saw the canvassers were working with the Bible Story company, he got really excited. "My grandchildren are doing Bible story skits, and we just pulled out our blue Bible story books and are reading through the stories again!" he said. Because of this encounter, he was willing to get *The Great Controversy*. After about forty minutes, Jennita was asked to leave, but she left the happiest canvasser that could be. Giants great and small—God is the slayer of them all!

I saw Jesus

Kristina Reeves often wondered what people thought when they saw the students dropped off and then praying together before going down the street. One evening, Cestmir dropped four canvassers at one spot. There were two streets, so two students per street. While they were praying, Kristina heard someone come out of a house near them and go back inside. What was that person thinking? She didn't have to wait long—the house was her first house!

A friendly man came to the door. He was Roman Catholic and said he enjoyed reading the Bible. He donated for a *Peace Above the Storm* and then started telling her about his devotional habits.

"One thing I have put into practice for a long time is finding Jesus in each day. Since I started, not a day has gone by without something reminding me of Him. Well, today I hadn't found it yet and was wondering if I ever would. Then, just a few minutes ago, I walked outside and saw you and your friends standing on the corner. At first I thought you were just some teenagers up to something, but as I looked closer, I realized that you were praying. I found it! In you four praying, I saw Jesus."

The locked door blessing

In the middle of the summer, Sheela Nadarajan's leader dropped her off in businesses for the morning. Four or five books went out in the first hour, so she was excited about what the day would hold. Her prayer request for the day was for God to teach her to trust in Him no matter what. She had no idea how He would answer this prayer, but with such a promising morning, she believed she would see the answer soon.

When Sheela's leader came to restock her with the book titles that she'd gotten out, she also moved her to a new strip of businesses. Sheela went out, eager to have more divine appointments. After being rejected at one business, she went to the next business. It seemed like a regular auto shop, so she walked in through the back, where she saw several employees. She started canvassing Joe, who quickly said he wasn't interested. Next, two other mechanics, Andrew and Mark, came over, so she showed them the books. Mark mentioned he was an atheist and wasn't interested in anything at all. Joe seemed embarrassed when Mark mentioned they were all atheist. He apologized and told Sheela to talk to Jim, who was in the little office in the garage. She showed books to Jim, who was slightly interested in the cookbook, but eventually he, too, said no. Jim told her to go inside to the main office and talk to Al and the receptionist.

At this point Sheela was a little annoyed because she was being re-directed to lots of different people. She took a deep breath and asked God for wisdom so she would know whether or not she was wasting her time at this business. She walked through the door that connected the garage and the main office, and was immediately taken aback by the beautiful display featuring four nice cars. It had opened into a huge showroom with several offices and bright lighting. Sheela wondered how she had missed the main doors and walked through the auto shop instead.

She found Al and canvassed him. He also was slightly interested in the cookbook but then told her he couldn't afford it. She canvassed the receptionist, who said she didn't have time. There were two young teenagers standing next to her, so she canvassed them. They declined the books but gave her a $7 donation, and she shared a pamphlet version of *Steps to Christ* with them. How discouraging! She had barely accomplished anything at that business. Sheela decided she needed to move on to the next business. Her favorite territory to canvass was the businesses, and since it was the last day in this town, she wanted to canvass as many as she could.

Sheela headed in the opposite direction from where she had come in—straight toward the main double doors. Then she prayed and asked God to help her remain cheerful and faithful. She approached the main doors and attempted to open them. One door didn't budge. She tried pulling open the other door. Same result. Now she was embarrassed, because she was unable to open the doors. She then tried pushing on both doors, but it was pointless. *Why in the world are these doors locked? It's the middle of the day. They should be open! How do customers get in here? This doesn't make any sense!* she thought. Sheela decided to try one more time, but her attempts were fruitless. The doors were still locked.

Sheela took another deep breath and let it out. *Now I am going to have to turn around and walk right past the people who already said no. How embarrassing,* she thought. Then she reminded herself that she had absolutely nothing to be ashamed of. She was working for the Lord, and that was a privilege and an honor. She turned around and walked past the receptionist and teenagers. As she was nearing the door that led to the workshop, Al stopped her and said, "I'll get your cookbook." He handed her $30, so she handed him the cookbook. Since his donation also covered another book, she showed him *The Great Controversy* and told him a little about the book. He thought it sounded interesting and mentioned that he would read it.

She walked through the door and was in the garage when Joe and Andrew stopped her and said they would like to get the DVDs. She was shocked! Joe got two DVDs, and Andrew ended up with one DVD and *Man of Peace*. Then Mark approached her and said, "I have eight dollars. Which book can I get?" She showed him *The Great Controversy*. Mark became interested in the book and mentioned that he was a history buff. He said he would read it when he had time, and that he would borrow the DVDs from Joe. They all thanked her for coming by and apologized for saying no the first time. She was shocked that all these books went out—especially to self-proclaimed atheists!

As Sheila walked away from the business, she paused on the sidewalk. She thought about what had just happened. A total of seven books had gone out in that business—*all because of the locked doors.* If the doors had been unlocked, she would have walked right out and gone on to the next business. She would not have had to walk past all those people again, allowing the Holy Spirit to nudge them into changing their minds about the books. She would have missed out on the blessing and the incredible way God revealed His power to her. She learned a valuable lesson in that business. She learned to wait on the Lord and trust in Him fully, despite the circumstances. She learned to not let pride get in the way of doing God's work. And until she gets to heaven, she'll never know why those doors were locked, but is so thankful that they were that day.

Faithfulness rewarded

"Even though there are only twenty minutes left, we should work until the end," David Armstrong and his friend decided.

The two were working with a Christian college that needed all of its other canvassers to fulfill other important evangelism functions, leaving only David and his friend out in the field for the day. After working all day, both were very weary. *Who would know if we quit a few minutes early?* David had been thinking. Temptations bombarded the tired soldiers. Yet, as nice as it sounded to quit early, neither of them felt that would be right. After all, it was God's work, and He deserves our all.

"Start here, and I'll drive to the other end of the street and work back toward you," David said while dropping off the other student.

Reaching the other end, he realized there were only enough houses for one person to do in that time. Turning back around, David wandered down the windy back roads, asking God to help him find a new location.

Soon David came upon a small group of townhouses. The first door he knocked on was a young single mother with a small child. She was interested in *Man of Peace* and the *My Friend Jesus*, but she did not have the money with her.

"Will you be around here for a few minutes? I need to run to the ATM. I'd really like to have these books."

"Sure," David replied.

He kept working, and the Lord blessed with more books going out at the next door. Soon the young mother returned with the suggested donation amount. He followed up with the survey, and she decided to sign up for Bible studies also.

A few weeks later, all of the students dispersed to join various summer canvassing programs, but before they left, they gave the Bible study contacts to two very faithful and dedicated lady Bible workers. To his joy, by the time the groups had returned to school, David received news that made his jaw drop. That young mother had taken Bible studies, and not only responded to them, but shared them with her sister and mother. Soon after, all three were baptized! God had certainly used those last few minutes of their day to start something beautiful in someone else's life.

The bar

One day Greg Davison's group was canvassing businesses, and on his side of the street was a walk-in bar. Nervousness crept into his mind as he approached it. One can never really know what to expect when canvassing a bar. Hesitantly, Greg walked into the store portion of the bar and began talking to the cashier.

After introducing himself, Greg began to tell the man, Nick, about the cookbooks they were offering and about a healthier lifestyle that he could be living. Nick's attention seemed to be more drawn toward the religious books Greg held. Greg first handed the cashier *Man of Peace* and next *Peace Above the Storm*. While this was happening, one of Nick's fellow employees walked up and joined the conversation.

The conversation eventually led to them asking questions about what Adventists believe. They also began to ask questions like, "Where is God when there is so much suffering?" and "What is the point in different religions?"

All of these questions sparked great discussion, and Greg told them about the local Seventh-day Adventist church they were working with and invited them to come to the service that their canvassing group was doing that Sabbath. Greg continued to tell them more about the books, and Nick said he was interested in the *Man of Peace* and *God's Answers to Your Questions*.

Before leaving, Greg asked to pray with Nick and his friend. They were very open to praying and requested prayer for their families and a greater knowledge of God.

When the prayer ended, there was a certain look that you see in people's eyes when you know that what was just said has touched them; and Nick had that look in his eyes.

It's crazy to see that when we most don't want to do something, that's when God has the greatest blessing in store for us. "For He has not despised nor abhorred the affliction of the afflicted; nor has He hidden His face from Him; but when He cried to Him, He heard" (Psalm 22:24).

Unexpected blessing

The whole evening had been full of quick rejections and hard-hearted neighbors. Feelings of discouragement started to rise as Jeandra Martin wondered if there was anybody who had a bit of kindness and wanted Jesus. Toward pick-up time she came to a long road, the end of which she couldn't even see, and was tempted to skip it.

I'm going to walk all that way just to get rejected, was her thought, but the Holy Spirit whispered to her to be faithful.

Turning into the first drive, she walked all the way down to the house only to find a grumpy elderly lady who shut her down. Walking back, she thought to herself, *See, Lord? I told You they wouldn't want anything.*

While these thoughts were going through her mind, a car turned into the road. As the car pulled up, the man driving rolled down his window and asked what Jeandra was up to. She started her canvass and ended up putting a whole stack of books in his car. His eight-year-old daughter was there, and they both worked through the different books and finally settled on a four-book set that was all message books.

Jeandra asked for any prayer requests at the end, and he shared that his uncle had a brain tumor, and it was really hard on all the family. After praying with them,

Jeandra walked away feeling rebuked that she had almost passed by this blessing. God used that experience to humble her and to teach her that His timing is perfect and that when He calls us to do something, it is in the best interest of others and ourselves to do it, even if at that moment it does not look like it.

Miraculous canine encounter

Laura Rupsaite rattled the fence. She nervously read an entertaining sign on the gate: "THIS DOG [picture of a Rottweiler] CAN GET TO THE GATE IN 2 SECONDS, CAN YOU?" Laura really liked dogs, but still. She rattled the fence again louder . . . nothing . . . she probed the latches on the gate, looked around . . . nothing . . . opened the gate and cautiously proceeded toward the house. Whew, all clear!

Halfway across the yard a full-grown German shepherd dog came tearing toward her from around the corner. He just let out one growl as he dashed at her with his facial expression leaving no doubt that he was going to tear her into pieces!

Laura tells the rest of the story. She says, "Now in moments like that, incredible amounts of information and calculations can pass through your brain very quickly and very distinctly! Running was definitely a futile option. No trees nearby that I could leap for. In that instance I saw five terrified faces watching from the window of the house, confirming to me that this dog meant business!

"I had entered this dangerous ground on the mission of the Lord, and now I realized that nothing less than God Himself could get me out of this one alive!

"A story that I had heard another colporteur share at a retreat involving a charging dog and a desperate prayer followed by an instant miraculous shutdown of the charge vividly crossed my mind. And with no other options or time left, I pointed my finger at the fast-approaching beast and shouted out exactly as my memory came to me of that experience: 'In the name of Jesus, shut up!'

"Instantaneously the dog came to a screeching halt, squealed at me, turned around, and ran back behind the house with his tail between his legs. It was as if it came to an invisible precipice just a couple of yards in front of me that it couldn't cross.

"I looked at the window. All the faces, now looking at me with their jaws down, took a moment before regaining composure and rushed to open the door for me to get in for shelter. A man came running from around the same corner of the house shouting, 'Are you OK?'

"Once inside, the wife and the children surrounded me and started asking what happened, gently scolding me for entering despite the warning. They told me that the dog was quite vicious to strangers, and that's why they had the signs up and the complicated latches on the gate. I remembered that it did take me diligence to figure out how to open that gate! They were so grateful, but baffled about what happened to the dog. Why did he stop the way that he did and run away instead of attacking?

"Once everyone calmed down, I proceeded to tell them why I was so persistent at getting to their house. They were amazed and almost spellbound by all the books I was showing to them. They ended up getting a bunch of books for their children and themselves, signed up for Bible studies, and sincerely thanked me for coming. After a prayer, they carefully led me out the side door of the house safely through a different gate."

What an awesome God we have who "rides the heavens to help you!" Literally! No powers of darkness can stop Him in pursuit of us.

The July Fourth special

It was the Fourth of July and 100 degrees in the shade. The day was wearing on; Jennita Schmidt had just approached a door, wiped the perspiration from her forehead, knocked on the door, and waited. A mother and daughter opened the door. The mother acted rather impatient and quickly turned down the cookbook.

"You are probably wondering what in the world these people are doing out on July the Fourth, right?" was Jennita's intuitive reply.

She laughed. "I guess so!"

"Well, this is the answer." Jennita pulled out *The Great Controversy* and handed it to the woman. "This is our July the Fourth special this year!"

The woman immediately flipped it over, read the back cover, and asked seriously, "Who do you believe the antichrist is?"

Her question came as a surprise. Not knowing what religion she was, Jennita was afraid to say the wrong thing.

"Well," Jennita said with a smile, "you would have to read it to find out!"

"But you must have an opinion!"

"Yes, but it is a serious question, and we cannot just take someone's word. It is something that we have to research and be convicted on for ourselves."

"I don't think I would read any of these books."

She handed all the books back, and the two began talking about their country and religion.

"Isn't it sad that so many problems in our world are done in the name of religion and are caused by people who claim to be Christian?" Jennita commented.

"I know. I am Catholic, and I know all the cruel things my church did in the past."

Not wanting to force any books on her that she had already rejected, Jennita offered the pamphlet version of *Steps to Christ*, and the woman went back into the house to get a donation.

When she came back with a generous donation, Jennita handed her *The Great Controversy*, saying, "I really would like you to have this book, although I will warn you that it does come from a Protestant perspective."

Again, Jennita was surprised by her answer: "You know I am Catholic, but well, I guess you could say, I am not really Catholic."

She seemed to be saying that she did not want to be pigeon-holed or judged as a Catholic and wanted to be seen as having an open mind. A searching Catholic who now had *The Great Controversy*! What a divine appointment!

Quick rejections, great timing

Ashley was sitting on the curb of the sidewalk with tears trickling down her face as her leader drove off. She felt defeated as she sat in the dark. The past two streets of houses had given more continuous rejection than she had ever experienced while knocking on doors. In less than half an hour the team would be picked up for the night, but Ashley's courage had departed. *I can't let Satan stop me from knocking on doors,* she scolded herself. She was upset about feeling like giving up, but she determined to get up and try again.

At the next house her voice was still weak and eyes still wet. The person was polite but not interested. As she continued to the next home, she saw several teenagers heading her way. Without waiting to meet them, she went to the door.

A young boy around age seven answered the door. As he closed the door to find his dad, one of the teenagers approached the same doorway. She began talking to him and put *The Great Controversy* into his hands. He became very interested in the book containing prophecy and last-day events, but he didn't have any money.

Just as it seemed that the teen's opportunity to get this book was slipping away, the young boy returned. He said that his dad was not coming out. Before he closed the door, the teenage brother told his younger brother that he wished he could get *The Great Controversy*.

"I have money!" said the young boy excitedly as he ran back into the house.

Because he was so young, Ashley thought he would return with only a few dollars, but to her surprise he returned with the exact amount for two books.

"Do you have anything for me?" the little boy asked eagerly. He chose *Your Pet and Your Health*, which includes messages about the state of the dead and God's love for us, as well as fun pet stories.

Just then, Ashley's leader reappeared with the team to pick her up. God had gained the victory of getting two messages into a home despite her setbacks. Had she not been rejected so quickly on the previous streets, Ashley would not have made it in time to meet those two searching young people. God's timing is perfect.

A need for healing

The wooden porch sagged dreadfully and uttered a creak of protest as Jaimie Douville stepped across its rotting planks to the front door. The walls shed old paint peelings of a dark, dismal color, and the ripped screen door, like a battered soldier, was held together by the iron bars across the front. No signs of life came from the deathly still house.

Does anyone even live here?

She knocked anyway.

Suddenly, a cacophony of noise erupted inside. Voices, pounding feet, and shrieks of an unidentifiable nature.

A heavyset woman struggled to the door, bombarded from behind by what Jaimie thought at first were dogs, begging to meet the tasty canvasser at the door. After a moment, though, she realized they were not dogs that fought to reach the door but children.

"Get *back!*" she shouted to the three blond-headed children. "I'm trying to *listen!*"

Jaimie could hear the frustration in the woman's voice, like a buildup of static electricity in the air. Her face was young, but her eyes portrayed a life that had aged her much too soon. She locked the metal screen door behind her and sat with Jaimie on the corroding gray armchairs on her porch. She looked at the books Jaime placed in her hands, though still somewhat distracted by the children wailing about who was at the door.

They continued speaking, and she began to relax and open up more.

Just then, her three children somehow managed to get out and surrounded Jaimie immediately. Jamie quickly turned her attention to the little ones, while the mother maintained rapt attention to the books.

"Whach yer name?" the little girl asked, her blue eyes sparkling expectantly. "I's Hannah." She put her warm fingers on Jaimie's arm, then her hand, and then her knee, as if wanting to investigate the stranger on her porch.

Haydon, the youngest, kept to himself and watched the proceedings with large, round eyes. He was three.

Hunter was the oldest, seven years old. He wore nothing but a diaper. "I don't know if he'll ever learn to use the toilet," his mother grumbled as she turned another page of the book. Hunter didn't seem to notice her comment.

"I lost two teeth," he showed Jaime with a wide grin. She spoke with him about his teeth, and they became friends immediately. Next, he brought her a fat black ant which, when he had placed it in her hand, had accidentally been smooshed to death in the process, so he took and threw it into the grass. When he couldn't find a flower, he brought her a pretty leaf.

The father came home just then, hot, irritated, and smoking a cigarette. He leaned on the porch for a few minutes to listen to the discourse, but then something happened. Jaimie didn't know if one of the children made a misstep or spoke a word out of turn, but suddenly the man erupted like a trembling volcano.

"Get in the house!" he shouted, one deadly finger pointed toward the dark innards of the house. The children scrambled around for a few minutes, wailing pitifully, trying to avoid the inevitable.

"No-o-o! I wanna stay outside!" they cried.

A battle of words ensued for several minutes as both parents attempted to herd their children inside, while still keeping a good face in front of their visitor. Finally, with the sniffling children locked behind the door and the father gone, the mother turned her attention back to Jaimie.

"I don't know what to do with them," she admitted. "They tell me they hate me. Once they locked *me* outside and said to never come back."

"You're a *bad* mom!" came the poisonous words from behind the rusty screen. She flinched a bit.

"I love you too." She tried to laugh it off, but her nervous chuckle only thinly veiled the frustration and despondency she felt. "They want to take my children away, but that won't help them. I was taken away from my parents when I was a child, and I don't want them to have to go through that. But it's so hard . . . I don't have any help from their father in raising them . . ."

Jaimie's heart filled with pity for her and her beautiful children. One mother, tainted by a less-than-ideal childhood, perpetuating the only thing she knew. Never had Jaimie seen a more miserable situation.

She pulled out *The Ministry of Healing* and opened it to the chapters about home influences and the mother's role. The desperate mother gripped the book hungrily, soaking up every sentence that she could.

"I wish I could have this," she said in desperation. "But I don't have the money. We live on food stamps, and I know my husband will not give me the money."

Jaimie urged her to try asking, but she returned empty-handed. "I can't get the books," she said, though she held them still.

Jaimie knew she had to go, but her heart longed to embrace the little family. She longed to introduce them to Jesus, the healer of bitter wounds, the binder of broken hearts. This woman was sincere, yet ever so damaged. Jaimie spoke to her words of encouragement that God brought to her mind. Then she placed *The Ministry of Healing* securely in her hands.

"Keep it," Jaimie told her. She knew she had extra donations to cover it.

The woman's face lit up.

"Thank you *so* much," she said emphatically. Jaimie could tell she meant it.

Jaimie prayed with the mother and went on her way that day, into the van, back to the church, into her safe, secure little sleeping bag surrounded by trustworthy and reliable people. But her mind remained with a hurting woman on the other side of the railroad tracks. What would become of her? At least Jamie had shared that book, and the Lord could work through it to reach that precious family for Him.

Jaimie shares, "I do this work because of people like her. This world needs the truth—the truth of what God can do for them *right now,* and the truth of what God is going to do very soon in this earth's history."

These people need truth, and the truth is begging earnestly for more workers to share it. What if God wants to use *you* to open the dark shades of some dismal soul? What if God wants to use *you* to introduce someone to Jesus?

"The youth literature ministry is the work for me," says Jaimie, "to reach people like her."

What if there are people at doors who would respond best to you, with your personality, with your strengths, with your life experiences, and with your passion for Him? What if you are the only person some people would connect with? Would you go? Or would you pass this life-changing experience by?

If you will go, He'll show you The Open Door.

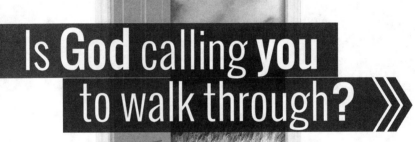

The
Open Door

For more infomation visit:
www.theOpenDoorBook.com